T0066516

An Exchange
of Love

First published by O Books, 2008
O Books is an imprint of John Hunt Publishing Ltd., The Bothy, Deershot Lodge, Park Lane, Ropley,
Hants, SO24 0BE, UK
office1@o-books.net
www.o-books.net

Distribution in:	South Africa
	Alternative Books
UK and Europe	altbook@peterhyde.co.za
Orca Book Services	Tel: 021 555 4027 Fax: 021 447 1430
orders@orcabookservices.co.uk	
Tel: 01202 665432 Fax: 01202 666219	Text copyright Madeleine Walker 2008
Int. code (44)	
	Design: Stuart Davies
USA and Canada	
NBN	ISBN: 978 1 84694 139 9
custserv@nbnbooks.com	
Tel: 1 800 462 6420 Fax: 1 800 338 4550	All rights reserved. Except for brief quotations in critical articles or reviews, no part of this
	book may be reproduced in any manner without
Australia and New Zealand	prior written permission from the publishers.
Brumby Books	
sales@brumbybooks.com.au	The rights of Madeleine Walker as author have
Tel: 61 3 9761 5535 Fax: 61 3 9761 7095	been asserted in accordance with the
	Copyright, Designs and Patents Act 1988.
Far East (offices in Singapore, Thailand,	
Hong Kong, Taiwan)	
Pansing Distribution Pte Ltd	
kemal@pansing.com	A CIP catalogue record for this book is available
Tel: 65 6319 9939 Fax: 65 6462 5761	from the British Library.

Printed and Bound by CPI Antony Rowe
www.digitalbookprint.com

An Exchange of Love

Madeleine Walker

BOOKS

Winchester, UK
Washington, USA

CONTENTS

Dedication

I would like to dedicate this book to my children, Sophie, Christopher and Cameron who have all helped me equally, in different ways, on my soul journey and to all my family, human and animal, past, present and future.
My deepest love always.

"Until one has loved an animal,
Part of their soul remains unawakened"

About the Author

Madeleine Walker lives in Somerset with her youngest son and their animals. She works as an animal intuitive and healer, horse and rider trauma consultant and empowerment coach and as a holistic stress management consultant for people.

She was previously married to a veterinary surgeon and helped run his practice, in the conventional field of veterinary medicine.

She later studied for her PGCE in adult education and taught many different groups from adults with drug abuse problems to those with learning difficulties. She has studied Art Therapy and psycho-neuro-immunology. She also works with Emotional Freedom Technique, EFT, which she performs by 'proxy' with animals and their human companions. Since her spiritual and intuitive awakening, her life has changed dramatically and she now runs workshops on animal communication and healing, emotional release through art and "Gateways to the Ancients", connecting to Egyptian and other ancient healing regimes.

She is passionate about raising people's awareness in understanding the animal's role in healing humanity.

Her work with animals and their owners has taken over from her previous teaching career and she now runs clinics and workshops throughout England and Wales and travels to many different countries to work with different species of animals in their natural habitat and also visits sacred sites around the world. She performs distant readings from hair samples and photographs, for clients who are geographically too far to visit.

She is a public speaker and columnist. *An Exchange of Love* is her first book.

Foreword

I have been so fortunate to have been able to work with Madeleine over the past few years and to call on her expertise in various cases that I just could not get to the bottom of. Giving these animals a chance to 'talk' about their problem allows them to unload anxieties, helps me in my choice of treatment for them and, very importantly, brings owner/carer and animal a much closer understanding in their relationship. This, combined with the healing offered by Madeleine, helps bring about a complete cure as we are able to get to the central disturbance in a case and thus treat mind, body and soul.

Many readers will be aware of the concept of past life and reincarnation and *An Exchange of Love* illustrates just how signif-icant past life experiences are to our animals' health in their current incarnation and how recognising and dealing with these issues, can help heal a sick animal and perhaps further enlighten their owners.

In this book, Madeleine Walker explores the often complex issues between an animal and its owner/carer which holistic veterinary surgeons such as myself, are meeting on a daily basis in the course of our work

This book will appeal to a wide range of readers from pet enthusiasts to professionals in animal care. Read and enjoy this book and be prepared to be amazed by the power of uncondi-tional LOVE.

Judith Webster

Prologue

A great number of people on the planet like to have a pet, and many more find inexplicable comfort in the company of an animal from another species. And beyond that, many also recognise that we have a spiritual connection with them. An Exchange of Love, the philosophy taught by me, goes even further. I hope to facilitate an awareness that the animals who share our lives are among our closest friends and have often been with us through many lifetimes in other incarnations, and that as our life long friends, they have access to parts of our subconscious that we ourselves are often too technological to tune into. Sometimes their attempts to draw attention to our deep seated discomfort this 'cry for help' can get them into trouble. Many times, when an animal 'misbehaves' to the point where the owner feels it necessary to summon help from a psychologist, an animal behaviourist or finally from a healer like myself, my communication with the pet reveals traumas that need healing, not only in the animal, but also in the owner. By knowing their human companion so well, the pet is able to 'flag up' a problem, deepseated within their owner that the person might not even have been consciously aware of, until it has been brought to their attention and explained through a session of animal communication.

The words, 'an exchange of love', represents the ability and willingness of one to heal another. This form of communication works on many levels. First there is the one-to-one link between myself and the animal on a physical and mental level. All I feel at this point is a giving and receiving of overwhelming love. When trust is established, even the most apparently aggressive and dangerous animal, relaxes, and the communication begins. This can throw up a complicated entanglement of issues, from trauma experienced by the animal in this life, or a previous one, to past life scenarios enacted with the same animal and same owner, that need to be revealed and healed. By constantly monitoring our energy levels, they may flag up presently undiagnosed health issues in their owner, or even be aware of incidents that have happened to the owner while they were away, causing them to return home in a negative state of mind, with 'jagged' energies attached to them which are sensed by the animals and have triggered the misbehaviour, as they have reacted to it.

The depth of their understanding, and the love and compassion with which they hold these concerns about our wellbeing, is not to be underestimated.

In this book I ask only that you open your hearts and minds. Set aside your doubt and skepticism – you may find the stories defy your expectations. During my lessons with my animal friends, I have often doubted my sanity and awaited the firm grip on my shoulder of the 'men in white coats' to take me to the asylum!

Yet the validity of their extraordinary depth of awareness is invariably confirmed afterwards once the messages have been relayed to the owner.

Allow the possibility of the animal's teachings. Detach from your fixed reality and open to unlimited possibilities. Some of the topics covered in this book may seem far-fetched.

The animals have come a long way to 'fetch' this enormous wisdom, to facilitate our re-awakening. Allow the accounts in this book to sow seeds of re-empowerment that will grow into understanding of the self.

The exchange is that we love our animals but not ourselves. Our animals teach us to trust ourselves and awaken us to remember that all is **one**. Their love for us has allowed them to not give up on us, despite their difficulty in reaching us.

We as humans have to let go of feelings of separation and reclaim our sense of self, to remember that there is only love. That is the animals' gift. They open us up to communicate with them, so that we can communicate with ourselves. We have drifted so far from our truth, the animals are here to gently nudge us back on our path of understanding. They have much to teach and we have much to learn. Everything we need to know is within us, but we have forgotten it along the way.

As you journey through this book, each chapter asks you to stretch your preconceived concepts to beyond your previous limitations. Allow yourself to remember how amazing you are...

Bon voyage!

Madeleine Walker

Introduction

The Somerset countryside was covered with a glistening layer of frost, and the grass stood in frigid rows, festooned with cobwebs that looked as if they had been crocheted by icy fingers. But that was outside. I was sitting, cradling a hot a cup of tea in my hands, basking in the warmth of my friend Leigh's farmhouse range. I'd retired to her kitchen after being outside in the cold, admiring her horses. I had shivered out there in the morning's chill wind, envying them their cosy rugs.

Sitting there in the snug kitchen, I couldn't resist the opportunity to sneak a quick cuddle with Sam, Leigh's new Jack Russell puppy. He was absolutely gorgeous and lolled his tiny frame around on my lap, lazily lying on his back whilst I tickled his perfectly pink tummy. I marveled at the softness of his skin and the wonderful puppy smell that should be bottled and sold for all animal lovers to enjoy.

I was drifting contentedly, when to my complete amazement Sam started to talk to me. I heard a voice in my head which sounded similar to mine, but seemed to be coming from somewhere outside of me. Sam's eyes were fixed intently on mine as though his thoughts and words were boring into me. He explained to me in a matter-of-fact way that he was a re-incarnation of Leigh's old dog, who had been a Border collie, and that he had come back to her in his Jack Russell body, to continue their loving relationship. I was so shocked that I nearly dropped him. I glanced over at Leigh, who was distracted, busily supplying a client with homeopathic remedies.

To avoid an accident, I thought it was prudent to put Sam on the floor whilst I recovered from my shock. This recovery was cut short as before my eyes, Sam's face sort of metamorphosized into the face of a Border collie to further illustrate to me what he had looked like in his previous incarnation. I knew what I was seeing, but it didn't make it any easier to comprehend. I could distinguish the black and white collie markings on the face and distinctive spots on its muzzle. This was getting weird! I was convinced I had finally 'lost the plot' and any proverbial marbles that I may have possessed had packed their bags and rolled out of the door! Then just as suddenly his face returned to his former tiny Jack Russell puppy youthful looks.

I was feeling rather stunned by Sam's revelation. Although I had been working on my psychic and intuitive abilities, this was something different. Leigh finally concluded dispensing remedies and her client left. She came back into her kitchen, apologising for the interruption, and chatted about this and that whilst I plucked up the courage to relate what Sam had told me. I finally felt that I had to tell her, so instead of asking her if she had once owned a Border collie, I just asked if she had ever owned a dog before. Leigh said she had not had a dog for years but she had adored her Border collie called Briar. She asked why I had asked the question and when I told her what Sam had said, she was just as astounded as I had been. But on reflection perhaps she could believe it, as Sam always seemed to know what was required of him and seemed to understand her so well. He seemed wise beyond his years and this had been commented on by many people.

I asked Leigh if she had a photograph of Briar, so she hunted for an old snap shot of her beloved Border collie and when she found one, there was Briar displaying all the distinctive markings that Sam had shown me.

I realised that this was something quite special. I had experienced past life regression, and recognised its healing potential in releasing trauma and emotional 'baggage', in helping us to understand where inexplicable phobias or negative self-belief patterns may originate from. Explorations of past lives also show how we travel in soul groups to act out different roles in different lifetimes to allow us to clear up unfinished business or unresolved issues. So after experiencing some of this, and reading a bit about past life therapy, I was quite open to the human aspect of this concept, but it had never dawned on me to question whether this might be possible for animals as well.

The concept that animals can actually choose to re-incarnate somewhere specific in order to continue the loving relationship with their owner, and commit to healing us on many levels, was astounding. I felt utterly compelled to relate my journey of awareness, to write this book to lead you through the stages of discovery and understanding, so that I could help others to appreciate just how much our animal companions have to teach us. So many animals are being re-homed, beaten, abused, abandoned and destroyed, because of their apparent behavioral problems. When we watch TV programmes about animals behaving badly, the problems are usually attributed to owners' mismanagement, consciously or otherwise.

There are some wonderful behaviourists, doing brilliant work, however the difference between their work and mine is that I connect directly to the animal telepathically. The animal will communicate on very deep levels, informing me of their connections with their owners and 'flag up' issues that need healing between the owner and the animal. This could be a past life issue that is impacting on a physical or emotional level, and the animals can sometimes 'mirror' stress in their owner. There has been a lot of research and documentation of the healing effects of owning a pet, but this is a much deeper concept.

Knowing how traumatic it is for animal lovers to lose a pet, I was very comforted by the fact that our beloved animal companions could return in another guise to continue the deep connections, and also by discovering that it was possible to receive such clear messages from these incredible creatures. The more I learnt, especially from horses, the more amazed I was at their insight into their owners and the deeper implications of their messages began to dawn on me; that there was an exchange, a two way healing. Animals so often displayed symptoms that appeared to need addressing, when the real reason for their treatment was to flag up an urgent problem in their owner's life.

It is truly wonderful to see how reassured my clients are now, when love and advice is given by their animals, and also to know that those animals care enough to be there again for their past human companions.

I am constantly amazed by my experiences and I am so honored to be trusted to delve into many very painful physical and emotional memories. I am humbled and privileged to be allowed to be part of a healing process and thank the universe for enabling me to devote my life to healing work. I realize that I have been given a wonderful gift. Not extra-ordinary powers unique to me, but the knowledge that there is so much more to our physical world than we ever imagined. That our animal friends possess the ability to give love unconditionally despite the cruelty that is imposed upon them sometimes. They can be our teachers. It seems that the only thing that is truly real is love. Love is not limited by a physical plane. It endures throughout eternity. We can all open our minds to acquire this gift. It is latent in every one of us. Animals and humans can give love, exchange love, receive and be healed through LOVE......

CHAPTER 1

Talking To Mulberry

When I reflect on the directions our lives have taken, it amazes me to notice all the steps along the way, which at the time seemed quite random. I believe that special animals are sent to us to help us on our life journey and they can be important catalysts in getting us back 'on track' if we have wandered from our life's purpose. One small goat radically changed my life and that of my youngest son Cameron, forever.

The profound change started when Mulberry was given to us in 1995 as a goatling, which is the term for a year old goat. This meant she was no longer a kid, but the age where goats behave like juvenile delinquents before they settle down to a more mature and manageable relationship with their owners. We owned a small-holding, with a strange menagerie of animals, including horses and ponies, dogs and cats, pet pigs, ducks and geese – always much too loved to be eaten!

I had bred pedigree British Alpine goats for a number of years and adored their vivacity and strong characters. Their glossy black summer coats that gleamed like ebony were a joy to behold. Unfortunately my other goatlings did not share my pleasure at receiving such a wonderful gift. They chased and harried Mulberry mercilessly. Goats, like any herd animals, like to ascertain their 'pecking order' and decide who's who in their hierarchy very quickly. This factor seemed to have played a large part in the development of Mulberry's character. She decided from then on, as she moved upwards as a member of our herd, that she would never be bullied again. If there was any bullying to be done, Mulberry would be the one to inflict disciplinary measures on any poor unsuspecting goat that had fallen foul of her favour.

My son Cameron was born in 1994 and so he and Mulberry were very nearly the same age. Mulberry was born in March and Cameron in May. As they both grew older, a strong bond developed between them. Cameron was never happier than when he had donned his Wellington boots and toddled alongside Mulberry in our paddock. She was a real harridan with other goats due to her unhappy start in the herd, but she was the epitome of gentleness with Cameron. Woe betide any goat that might have inadvertently bumped him, Mulberry would immediately rush to his defense! On summer days Cameron was as picturesque as a fashion accessory, as he clung to Mulberry, arms draped around the nanny goat's neck. They would both blissfully meander around the field as Mulberry searched for tasty morsels to eat. Cameron's golden ringlets of hair shone in the sunlight, as dressed in his T-shirt, shorts and wellies, he went striding out the best way his little legs could, alongside his faithful friend. When Mulberry's own kid, Peak, once knocked Cameron over, Mulberry dealt severely with her misdemeanors by biting her offspring's ear, causing her to bleat in complaint. A larger goat was on the receiving end of a similar punishment as Mulberry exerted her authority in defense of her young human ward.

We often remarked on how at home little Cameron was within the herd. He would find a bit of stick in the orchard and gently tap the goats on the back and, ironically, we imagined him as some ancient herdsman. He was always gentle and calm with them. Little did we realize that he was re-enacting and drawing on his past life experiences.

Poor Mulberry had experienced great difficulties when she gave birth to her first set of twins. I put it down to just being her first time, but sadly she became very distressed again, the second time she tried to deliver her kids. Her labour was prolonged and she seemed to be fading, so I called the vet, who admitted her for an

Cameron and Mulberry

emergency cesarean. Poor Mulberry was in a desperate condition. The vet managed to deliver a live female kid, but Mulberry was in a very bad state when we got her home. She was so weak that I banked straw bales around her to support her, placing her kid next to her, separated by bales, protecting it from injury if Mulberry fell or tried to move. I hoped that seeing her kid might give her the will to live.

I sat up hour after hour, for nights on end, trying to persuade her to eat or drink something. Her flesh melted from her. I was so desperate that I frantically tried to remember what I had been taught about the healing energy in our hands, not really believing I could save her. She looked so pathetic, a bag of bones, her glorious black coat dulled and lacklustre. Mulberry dying was not an option. How could I tell Cameron his best friend in all the world had died! I prayed so hard for help. I placed my hands around her and ran them alongside the massive wound that looked like a bizarre Zip on her hollow side. Suddenly I felt heat pouring out of my hands and felt guided to place them at different parts of her body. I knew I was being helped and guided. I jokingly said to Mulberry, "I'll kill you if you die on me!" I couldn't bear the prospect of telling Cameron that she had gone. Indeed she had become such an integral part of the family that we were all desperately worried about her and would all be inconsolable if she died.

Somehow she began to claw her way back to health. It was a slow process. The only liquid she would drink was the warm water that I poured onto porridge oats. She licked the warm milky fluid and as she gained strength she managed to slurp up the soggy oats. Sometimes she would inhale some oaty gruel up her nostrils and she would sneeze and coat my face with a splattering of oatmeal, which under other circumstances might have been quite efficacious to my complexion, so I used to return from the goat shed sporting a very strange pebble-dashed appearance!

Finally after three months of intensive loving care, Mulberry began to look and act her old self. She exerted her authority and discipline, which she obviously felt she had been neglecting of late, exacting her revenge on any careless behavior by her caprine associates. Mulberry resumed her place as Queen of the herd and our respect grew for her courage and will to live after such an ordeal.

Cameron continued to spend many happy hours with Mulberry. Although he was a wonderful child, his father and I struggled as he never seemed to be able to settle at night. We endured years of disturbed nights and his idiosyncrasies increased. We used to joke that we must have performed some serious misdemeanor in a past life in order to have to struggle so much with Cameron in this life. We both adored him, but his behavior away from the animals was beginning to take its toll. He developed an obsession with railway engines and model railways, which was obviously quite normal for little boys. However, his next obsession made us question whether all was well emotionally and mentally. He became fascinated by telegraph poles. He could describe in detail, every pole on our four mile journey to school and attempted to draw them with pieces of paper spread across our lounge floor. If he had drawn one wire thicker than it should have been, instead of replacing that piece of paper or altering the picture of the offending telegraph pole, he erupted in a tidal wave of frustration and anger and abandoned the whole project in fury.

We were naturally concerned, as he seemed to put so much pressure on himself, and became so distressed. This obsession was beginning to affect his life; he was teased at school about the way he waxed lyrical about the poles, and he couldn't understand why no-one else seemed interested. We had to construct some 'poles' in our garden and our patience was tried to the extreme when he became so pedantic about the exact curve or level or the 'wires' we made with rope tied to wooden posts. These attempts to create replicas of his favourite poles were deemed unsatisfactory, much to our exasperation.

When Cameron was seven years old, I was asked to attend a seminar on Autism and Aspergers Syndrome. I had never heard of Aspergers, but from the description of some of the symptoms, my ears began to prick up as I thought that although Cameron's issues seemed quite mild, there were definitely recognizable tendencies. I thought this could possibly explain his strange obsessions. We consulted doctors and pediatricians and discovered that this was the case, and although Cameron managed incredibly well, it was challenging to support him in a way that made life as happy as possible for him. As long as he could be with Mulberry he was content.

The turning point came when a therapist I had consulted thought Cameron was suffering from a past life trauma. This was a bit of a shock, and when she described what she intuited about the cause of Cameron's death in this past life, my blood ran cold. It was so awful yet it did somehow, bizarrely, explain some of his fears that were unfounded in this life. She told me how, in the early eighteenth century, Cameron had been locked in a very dark small room or cupboard. He had been about six years old. He had been rather naughty and the man who was his guardian had placed him in this awful dark place to rethink his behaviour. Cameron had been so frightened and horrified by his plight that he had vomited and then choked. To the complete chagrin of the man, when he went to enquire whether Cameron had learnt the error of his ways, it was too late to revive him. I didn't know what to think about this strange and horrifying information. It chilled me to the bone, but it also seemed far-fetched. However, when I discussed this possibility with Cameron's father, he reminded me of some of Cameron's first words. Apart from the usual, "Mum,

Mum, Mum, Dad, Dad, Dad," he used to stand in front or our large cupboard and say, "In a dubber, in a dubber!" This had continued for a number of weeks. We had no idea at the time what he was referring to or what on earth he was trying to say in his diminutive way. Christopher, his older brother translated for us, "He's saying in a cupboard! In a cupboard!" I had forgotten all about this incident, so it really made us rethink all the evidence that might prove this past life trauma tale to be valid.

Cameron always became completely hysterical if he was left or even laid in a room on his own. He would work himself into such a frenzy that he would vomit. He would then start to choke. He would make terrible choking sounds if ever he became stressed and thoroughly abhorred any confined dark places. The prospect of just 'allowing him to cry himself to sleep', as we were advised, was not an option. I had experienced mild 'grizzles' from my other children, when laid in a cot, and then they would settle contentedly as we monitored their peaceful sleep. Not Cameron. He displayed abject terror. For years he either shared our bed or we played 'musical beds' all night; anything to get at least *some* sleep. Eventually we sought help from complementary therapists. Homeopathy and Cranial Sacral therapy did much to alleviate his symptoms, but we only finally managed to get a full night's sleep when Cameron was about eight years old.

Through all this, our beloved animal companions shared their lives with us, with Mulberry always dominating the proceedings. She was always the constant in our chaotic midst. She continued to be a life support and confidante for Cameron, and if I'm honest, for myself, too. She seemed so wise and omniscient, placidly chewing the cud as though contemplating life's dilemmas and challenges. Apart from one occasion when she nearly hanged herself between her stable doors whilst striving to steal some tasty vine leaves growing around them, she maintained a condescending and superior countenance. There was nothing quite like snuggling into Mulberry's soft furry neck, breathing in her reassuring, gentle goaty aroma, far removed from the pungent 'pong' of her male counterparts. There were many occasions when I sought relief and succour from life's turmoil by having a cuddle with Mulberry. I understood why Cameron found such contentment in the simple pleasure of being in her company.

We moved house several times due to work and schools, and finally had to reduce our herd of goats and decided that it was only really practical and manageable to just keep Mulberry. We found knowledgeable and loving homes for our remaining goats and Mulberry was installed in our new home, which had a large garden and a stable. Although I would never keep any other herd animal singly, she seemed to prefer human company and always enjoyed dominating our dogs, cat and hens with her iron hoof. As long as there was plenty of activity for her to oversee, she was happy. We even named our new house "Mulberry Cottage" as when I had recounted the benefits of this house when viewing it for the first time; I had said there were fantastic facilities for Mulberry. My friend asked if it was also suitable for people. We laughed as I said the only thing I didn't like about the house was the name, so it was suggested to rename it in Mulberry's honour.

All this time my work as a healer and a teacher was developing. I began to facilitate healing groups. I ran empowerment sessions and workshops from various venues and from home. I had recognized what it felt like to be disempowered and I wanted to help people reclaim their sense of self. There were so many twists and turns in the meandering journey that my life took.

Cameron struggled at his schools and was often bullied. He was deemed 'slow' in his lessons, which we knew was a complete fallacy. We decide to somehow manage to send him to a private school where his confidence could be raised and his abilities recognized. He was extremely methodical and terrified of making mistakes, which was why it took so long for him to complete his work. Unfortunately, this was very expensive, and our combined wages could not support our large house and Cameron's schooling. So we decided to downsize and moved to a semi-detached cottage with three acres near Cameron's new school.

All our animals were installed in their new home, and life continued for a few weeks. Mulberry as usual was the kingpin, receiving many visitors and titbits at her gate, as passers by admired her.

As the summer wore on Mulberry began to show her age. We had been **Cameron and Troy** given a lovely old horse called Troy by a wonderful shaman called Dave. These two new characters in our life proved to be vital catalysts. I had been introduced to Dave by Leigh, who had seen him at work healing horses with cancer in Cornwall. I had asked for his help in treating my mother, who had become seriously ill. He was a great support, and I have learned so much from him. The first time I saw Troy and heard that his nickname was Plod I burst into tears. This was quite embarrassing as nobody could understand my emotional outburst. I just 'knew' that Troy was a horse that I had owned 25 years earlier in his previous incarnation. He had been a very similar looking coloured cob called Mister Plod. I had been deeply saddened at his loss.

There was something so deep in Troy's eyes that went right through me. I wished I could give him a happy retirement when the time came and I thought he would be a lovely companion for Mulberry. However Dave had other plans for him, but these were to change, unbeknown to me, as somehow the universe contrived to place Troy in our home.

Cameron and I had returned home from our holiday and found a message on our answer phone from a mutual friend, saying were we interested in having Troy, as Dave needed a good home for him. We called back immediately and a couple of weeks later, the old boy arrived, his large feathered hooves clomping down the tail board. Troy, whose rotund corporation, reminding him to access the nearest food source, immediately set about munching the grass. Mulberry's initial reaction was one of terror. She was horrified to find this huge, hairy, horsey vision in her yard, where she had happily reigned supreme.

Troy and Mulberry became great friends and were always playing tricks on each other, trying to get each other into trouble. I would complain at Troy fidgeting whilst I picked out his hooves. I would remonstrate with him as his great hairy feet where quite heavy to hold up and his jerking movements jarred my back. However, it was Mulberry who was the agent provocateur. I caught her tweaking large mouthfuls of hair from Troy's woolly coat because she was jealous of the attention I was giving him. She was even more pleased that he should be chastised instead of her. She was such a character and always up to mischief and making me laugh. Gradually, however, she began to slow down and become quite creaky in her joints. She just seemed to lose her sparkle.

When I returned from spending a week in Egypt expanding my awareness of ancient energies, I discovered a large tumour in her chest. She had also rapidly been afflicted by rot and awful deterioration of her hind hoof. Pedigree goats do not manage the same longevity as crossbred and scrubland goats, as they are bred to produce copious amounts of milk. Much of their vigour goes into milk production. Those factors and her physical traumas in the past took their toll. I felt that she was telling me she'd had enough, that it was time to go. I do feel that animals can show us when they are ready to pass. When I asked her telepathically, she told me that she wanted to go as she was very cross she couldn't get around as freely as she used to. I rang our vet for advice. For all our sakes I wanted to be sure I was doing the right thing.

I was devastated at yet more loss for Cameron to cope with after a very traumatic time of family problems. I was dreading approaching the subject with him. I knew only too well what he had been through that year and how hard it had been. However, he realized that Mulberry was not happy in her condition and we had a long talk about the responsibilities for the life and well-being of the animals in our charge, but also tragically sometimes we had to be responsible for their deaths, to free them from their suffering.

Cameron had a horror of the thought that Mulberry would be shot. He thought that if this awful deed had to be done, an injection would be best. I knew from previous experience that this was not always the best course of action with goats. I decided to get Cameron to talk to our vet. He agreed that he would respect the vet's advice as he had great faith in her abilities. She advised that the hunt kennel-man would use a humane killer which took the form of a bolt, and that it would be best for Mulberry as she hated injections.

I was astounded at Cameron's bravery; he loved his goat so much he knew he couldn't allow her to suffer. I told him that their deep love for each other would never, never die. I reassured him that she would always be there for him and that true love never disappears, it is there for eternity, and she would always be in his heart. So it was decided. I booked the kennel man to come on the Monday morning when Cameron was at school. We had a very emotional weekend with lots of cuddles with Mulberry, and lots of her favourite treats. She had a passion for banana skins, and to this day I can never throw out or recycle a banana skin without thinking of how cross she would be at the waste. She had a birthday cake every year where banana skins were the main ingredient.

I shall never forget Cameron's last farewell to Mulberry as he left to go to school. He was so brave, which in a way made it harder for me as I fought back my tears. Somehow we got to school and had big hugs and I told him that I would tell him how everything had gone when I collected him later. I placed Troy in the lower paddock as I didn't want him to witness his friend's death. I heard the screech of the kennel man's brakes and I knew the time had come. Trying to summon up every ounce of my fading courage, I led him to Mulberry's yard. He was such a kind young man, so sympathetic. He was so calm and gentle with Mulberry, talking to her and stroking her softly. To my horror he produced a gun and placed a bullet in it ready to perform his dreadful task. I didn't know what to do – I had promised Cameron that this wouldn't happen, but I knew it was the right thing to do. That excruciating bang went right through me. The tears streamed down my face... our wonderful friend was dead. Could our lives become any worse? There had been so much loss and grief that year. I was so grateful that the young man had shown such compassion for Mulberry and me.

Somehow I composed myself to visit a friend of mine who was using me as a 'body' for an energy healing course that she was studying. She was very kind and totally understood how hard it is to lose such a beloved friend. I was lying on her therapy couch as she worked on my body. Suddenly, deep in meditation, I saw Mulberry lying where she had fallen when she was shot. Her spirit jumped up, shook her head and proceeded to frolic around the yard, something that she hadn't managed physically for a long time. She told me that she was so happy to be free of pain and could now do whatever she wanted and be just as mischievous and loving as ever. This vision was so wonderful and cheered me greatly. Even though I am totally convinced and have had so much evidence that there is life after death, it doesn't make it any easier to bear at the time.

I collected Cameron from school and told him about the day's awful events, omitting the part about the gun and the bullet as I knew he would be devastated. He was reassured when I described my vision, where Mulberry had shown me she was fine. I reiterated that their love connection was so strong, and she would always be there for him. I profoundly hoped that this was true. This ten year old boy had shown more courage in the last year than many adults would have managed, and I was so proud of him.

However, two nights later, as I was getting him ready for bed, I was stunned by his outburst. He glared at me with such shocking fury. "How could you!" he bellowed "How could you have lied to me." I had no idea what he was talking about. He was distraught. I pleaded with him to explain what I had done wrong and why he was so angry with me. His next words shook me to the bone, as he shouted, "Mulberry told me that there was a bullet in her head, and that she was shot!"

I couldn't believe it, I begged him to forgive me, and told him that I really didn't know the kennel man was going to shoot her. I tried to reassure him that it had been very quick and that she wouldn't have felt any pain. Then I realized the enormity of what had transpired. Mulberry had not only communicated with Cameron from spirit with devastating accuracy, but he had heard her messages all too clearly. I tried to comfort him by showing him that Mulberry had proved she was still around him and that she was still there for him to call upon to help and support him.

I don't feel that time necessarily heals grief, I feel we find coping strategies in order to continue our lives. I draw great comfort from our spirit allies, but there is nothing that can replace a physical hug, although our loved ones do their best from spirit to comfort us.

Cameron talked to Mulberry most days, and she continued to give him amazing evidence that she was very much aware of what was going on in his life. Whenever he had a difficult exam at school, he took in a photograph of him holding one of Mulberry's birthday cakes as she devoured it with relish. He felt that she was with him somehow, supporting and encouraging him to be confident in his abilities. She truly helped him realize his strengths through some of the challenges of Aspergers.

Mulberry taught us to believe in communication and support from spirit. She has proved time and time again that her love for Cameron is undying. She has reassured him on many occasions when he has been fearful and has proved correct in her explanations. Sometimes, when I have a difficult case that is puzzling me, we consult Mulberry, and Cameron tells me what is needed.

A short while after Mulberry's death, I was contacted by a client, who had just received a call from her parents. They had told her that a pony had been dumped on the motorway near their farm and the police had placed the pony in their field. They had no idea where the pony had come from or what had happened, but it was in a poor condition physically and emotionally. I asked Cameron to consult Mulberry and she gave him a plethora of information, especially about the pony's physical condition, age and history which the vet verified when he visited the farm to examine the pony. She even told us that the pony's name was Rosy. We had no way of proving that, but she did seem to answer to the name and is now fully recovered and happy, though her previous irresponsible owner has never been traced.

Troy has also proved to be a wonderful ally for Cameron and I. He told Dave, who gave him to us, that there was something wrong with Cameron's thought processes. Dave rang me to question this as he was concerned by what the old horse was telling him. I disclosed that Cameron had Aspergers, and he exclaimed, "Oh that's what the old boy was trying to tell me." He went on to say that Troy had told Dave that he really liked it when Cameron placed his hands on his left shoulder as he has very healing hands. I encouraged Cameron to do this and it became obvious that Troy responded to Cameron's newly rediscovered healing abilities. I will describe later how Troy has helped on many difficult cases. Cameron often accompanies me when I visit horses and his psychic abilities are amazing. I feel that his

Aspergers in some way helps him to view things in a non-formal method, and he can intuit information in a special way.

He has grown so much from all our emotional hardships and that through his grief he has learnt vital lessons about healing and love. I also know that he has led me down this unconventional path and that we have been together many times before. He has confirmed my beliefs that we are all connected. Both humans and animals travel in 'soul groups' and we interact together many times to learn and evolve on our soul's journey.

Mulberry's Story

One Sunday morning, Cameron and I were having a lazy lie in. He snuggled down in the bed as we chatted. We had been talking about the concept of past lives and how deep connections and attachments to people and animals could continue through lifetimes. That we might time travel in a sort of soul family, playing different roles as if characters in a play, resolving our differences, learning lessons and continuing loving relationships. I had told him the story of Sam the Jack Russell puppy who had come back to help Leigh, and Cameron wondered if he had had a past life with Mulberry. I said we could see if he might remember and he nonchalantly agreed. I asked him to take some deep, gentle breaths and imagine walking down a long staircase. When he had reached the bottom, I asked him to imagine a door and that on opening the door it would be filled with light and he would step through into another time. As he stepped through the door he was astonished to find that he was black – a small boy of about seven years old. I asked him to examine his appearance and he described his diminutive frame. The more he described his experiences, the more I was able to experience and to share the images that were unfolding as if watching a video clip. It was as though he was giving me a running commentary on what we were both 'seeing' in this past-life flashback. Although the emotions felt were quite intense, it was as though he was experiencing and observing at the same time. He described the events in a calm, matter of fact way, without fear, just feeling wonder at the unfolding connections.

The relentless African sun beat down on the parched land. The huge crocodile waited…. he waited for the inevitable vibration of hooves that would gingerly find their way to the water's edge. The crocodile lay almost somnolent like a lazy log, effortlessly poised, for just the right moment to launch his expert attack. Such skills had been used for millennia and he was a master of his trade.

The diminutive Bantu boy randomly waved a crooked stick at his depleted and scrawny goat herd, as he drove them towards the river. The drought had been cruel this year and many of the older milkers had succumbed to the harsh conditions. The boy knew full well of the dangers of this river. He knew what lay patiently waiting, caught up in their own cycle of survival, but the tribe's ancient well had become sour and diseased. The river was their only hope of hydration and the herd was desperate, especially the old milker, who had just kidded. She had struggled to deliver her female kid and the boy had deftly used his small hands, to reach inside the goat and realign the misplaced leg that had been causing an obstruction. The kid was weak and struggled to stand for a few hours after her birth. The boy felt sorry for the kid's harsh introduction to a world of strife. He had carried the kid in his arms to relieve its struggle in the art of walking, until it had gained strength and was now able to totter alongside her mother. She was very pretty with unusual markings and he was proud of his skill as a herdsman, but understood even at his tender age, the sometimes cruel reality of the world he lived in.

The herd tentatively placed their hesitant hooves into the soft mud at the water's edge, the goats at the rear, bleating in their thirsty frustration. The sweet smell of the females mixed with the rank odour of the large dominant male, whose beard drooped in the mud as he drew closer to the water he so desperately needed. As the goats at the rear pushed forward, several at the front were forced into the water. The mother of the kid splashed in panic as though she realised, too late, her impending fate. The huge reptile lunged into action from his repose and grabbed her foreleg just above the knee. The impact jettisoned her into the water, her cloven hooves flailing in the air as she struggled to escape its vice like grip. The kid was left soaked and shivering in confusion at the water's edge and was in danger of being thrust into the water to meet the same fate, as other crocodiles joined the fray. The boy charged forwards screaming at the herd, risking his safety by driving the goats away from the edge, and scooped up the sodden, terrified kid bleating desolately for its mother. Sadly she had now disappeared beneath the surface with only some ominous bubbles betraying her dying presence beneath the water.

The young boy stood trembling from the shock of the lightening speed of the attack. He screamed and shouted as he watched the large crocodile rolling and twisting the flesh from the unfortunate goat. Another crocodile hissed angrily at the boy and eyed the skinny legs and small bare feet that charged up and down the river bank, desperately trying to claim a foot hole in the churned mud.

Eventually the panicked herd withdrew from the river. An older boy from the tribe, hearing the commotion, ran down to help drive the goats away back to the prickly kraal and the thatched huts that barely protected the tribe from their tribulations. The boys were fearful that other predators might be attracted by the smell of fear and death. Lions and hyenas were just as desperate to survive in this cruel drought.

The small boy cuddled the kid. He'd been remonstrated by one of the elders for losing yet another valuable asset of the beleaguered tribe. The soft fur, warm body and dainty dangling hooves, somehow gave the boy solace as they had to look to each other for comfort now. As the kid had no mother the boy would have to hold another milker so that the kid could suck and learn to duck any angry reprimands from the surrogate mother. And this is how the kid survived. Somehow they managed to scrape some moisture and nourishment from the parched landscape. The boy gained a deep attachment to the kid and she would follow him whenever she could, bleating loudly if he should disappear from sight. They somehow sought succour in each other. There had been other orphan kids, but this one was different. The boy's father had been killed in tribal conflicts and his mother was weak with fading health. He felt very alone in the world, the other goats were a source of worry and weight of responsibility, as he was usually blamed for any misfortunes. This kid showed some hidden strength and will to live which gave him a message of hope somehow. A deep bond of love developed, something the small boy had very little experience of previously, which made their relationship even more special.

Six months passed and the rain had finally quenched the land. The kid was old enough to be weaned from milk and the next year would be able to have kids of her own. The boy was proud of his care and how well she had managed to survive, despite adversity. They still spent as much time together as possible. She was always at his side when the herd was grazing on the precious green shoots and leaves on the thorny bushes.

One fateful night, the boy was awakened by terrified shouts and animals screaming. He had fallen asleep inside the kraal. A warring tribe had come to attack the men and steal the herds of cattle and goats. Huts were burned and those that didn't manage to escape were slain. The small boy tried to hide the kid in the thick bushes but in her fright she ran out into the main herd, which was then driven by the attackers. The boy was so frightened and knew his fate if he were caught by these ruthless tribesmen. He had to watch in dismay as his herd was driven away, taking his only friend. Tears poured down his dust streaked face as he strained his eyes in the darkness, to see if he dared follow. He decided to wait until sunrise. There was a deep ache in his chest – the pain of loss. The horror of the assault on his pathetic village consumed him. His mother had barely survived and looked frailer than ever. Everywhere seemed to be left in smoldering ruins, and without the sustenance of the cattle and goats, which had all been taken, there was little hope for the future of the tribe. Once the sun began to show its force, the boy set off, following the spoor. He didn't know what he was going to do if he found the missing herd, but he just knew he had to try to find his caprine friend and rescue her. He followed the trail of hoof-prints and dung, mixed with evidence of their captors. The boy was so hungry as most of their maize meal had been stolen or spoiled and there was no meat or milk now that the animals were gone. He knew his plight was desperate, but he couldn't just give up. Finally, when he felt that his legs would no longer be able to carry him, he pushed through the undergrowth and there in the distance was the marauding tribe's kraal. He could see that several of the goats and cattle were being slaughtered and he caught a brief glimpse of his little goat being chased around by older boys, which enraged him. There was a soft growl behind him; in his haste to recover his lost friend, he had failed to notice other prints in the soft earth. The lion's kill was quick and merciful, the small boy died instantly, never again to feel the warm, soft fur and sweet smell of his only friend.

Cameron lay blinking with an expression of mild surprise, but he was quite calm as he lay next to me. I had gently brought him back to the present and we were amazed at what had occurred. He felt he had been very brave, endeavouring to rescue the goat and to care for her the best he could. He reflected that Mulberry had tried to repay him in this lifetime. She had somehow rescued him from his challenges and tribulations, in helping him to cope with his life. She had also reawakened his telepathic, intuitive skills and given him the tools to prepare him for maturity. She had given him so many gifts.

I told Cameron that there had never been a time when our lives had not been filled with animals. I recounted the times when I had spent many happy school holidays on a relative's farm. My brother and I rode ponies and learnt to milk cows and goats and I had been given a kid when I was young. We were very fortunate to have shared our childhood with so many wonderful animals, dogs, cats, rabbits, hamsters, mice and guinea pigs.

I told Cameron I wanted my children to have the same fun and joy of an informal, if slightly chaotic upbringing. I felt that learning to care for animals taught vital lessons of responsibility and care for others. I wanted my children to experience the unconditional love of a dog, the thrill of riding a horse, to cuddle a cat or to have a mouse hide in your sleeve. So I contrived to always be lucky enough to have special animal companions as part of our extended family.

CHAPTER 2

Our Spirit Animal Friends

Having discovered how our animals can still continue to help us, even after their death, I was surprised to find that they could also help in my healing sessions with their human companions. The first time this startling revelation occurred was when, on a sunny morning in Devon, my healing room became rather 'crowded'.

Duke the Shire horse

Bert hobbled into the room. Speaking in his wonderfully soft Devon brogue, he explained some of his symptoms and the pain that they were causing his body. As he cautiously sat down, I observed his energy and general physical appearance. His ruddy complexion and gnarled hands betrayed his hard working conditions that he had endured over the years. He seemed tired and careworn. As he described what had been happening to him physically, I felt a great sadness in him emotionally and a frustration at his perceived rapid passing of the years. I intuited feelings of anger at himself, for no longer being able to do the work around the farm as he used to. He was gradually being forced to hand over the running of the farm to his son. Instead of taking the opportunity to enjoy some well earned rest, it seemed he was punishing himself to still endure a heavy workload that was taking its toll on him physically and emotionally, as he was beginning to realize his limitations. He was worn out.

I suddenly saw the most enormous horse's head behind him. It was just the head but quite animated nonetheless. It was black with a large white blaze down his face, which then became pink as it reached his lovely soft muzzle. It was so clear, I felt if I leant a little closer I would smell him. His whiskery chin nodded as if he desperately wanted to convey some important information.

I was rather taken aback to see this apparition so clearly behind Bert. I found it difficult to concentrate on what Bert was saying, as the horse was nodding even more violently, and I could feel his frustration at not being discussed or recognized.

Eventually I felt so pressured by the horse, I had to stop Bert's dialogue and somehow explain what I was 'seeing'. I asked Bert if he recognized the huge horse and described his whiskery face. I thought that Bert would think that I was the one who might need treatment, but instead he said "Ah that'd be Duke".

Apparently Duke had been a Shire that Bert had known when he was a young lad growing up on his father's farm. Duke 'showed' me a picture in my mind, of how Bert had worked the giant horses even as a small boy, spending hours toiling in the fields. Duke had been very special. Even though he had towered over the young boy as he struggled to hold the plough, his great feathery hooves had always kept a steady, straight furrow line. Duke always did his best to help Bert complete a good day's work, even in the harshest elements. No modern mechanical machinery to aid the farming processes back then. Although Bert found the work very demanding he loved the horses and especially Duke.

Duke showed me a scene where there was a severe hoar frost and I saw both horse and boy's laboured breath, billowed out into the cold air. It was a wonderful scene from a bygone age. I asked Bert what had become of Duke. His expression saddened. He said that in those days animals had to earn their keep and if they were no longer financially viable, they would no longer be kept. He still remembered his distress when one day, he discovered that Duke was no longer waiting in his stall munching contentedly. Whilst Bert had briefly left the farm for a family visit, his father had taken the opportunity to have Duke destroyed. Bert had been heart-broken and there had never been a horse that had replaced Duke in his heart. He had worked and ridden many horses since those days but Duke was the one that remained his favourite. Of course, as he grew older Bert realized the practicalities of making a farm pay and that they could not afford any 'passengers' and understood his father's hard decisions.

In his turn he had married and taken over the farm, deep in the Devon countryside. He never seemed able to relax and switch off from the demands of the farm and so eventually he was wearing himself out. Duke wanted Bert to be able to have the time to enjoy his later years and make the most of his remaining life.

Duke told me to tell Bert that he should take the opportunity now to do all the things that he loved, but never previously had the time for. Duke wanted Bert to have the happy retirement that he was never allowed.

Bert was never very good at taking anybody's advice on such matters, but because Duke had been so vehement, he agreed to give the matter careful thought. At this Duke nodded again, but this time with pleasure at his old master's acceptance of his help.

Just as suddenly as Duke had appeared behind Bert, he disappeared, to be replaced by the spirit of a Jack Russell terrier. I described the colour and markings to Bert, who to his credit, seemed quite un-fazed by my strange visions and said he recognized the dog.

Bert said that this little terrier had belonged to his wife before they had married. The dog apparently had been a very effective chaperone, in the days when prenuptial fraternizing was frowned upon. If Bert had been too free with his affection, the dog would growl and defend his mistress' honour, much to the annoyance of Bert! However, once they were properly married, the dog begrudgingly had to accept that his mistress had divided loyalties.

I thanked the spirit animals for their help in this session. I worked to alleviate some of the physical symptoms with Bert and we discussed the messages from the animals who had tried to help us. I reiterated the solemn message from Duke that Bert needed to look after himself and enjoy life. The terrier's presence had been to remind Bert of fun times in the past and that he could now spend more time with his wife and rediscover their joint interests away from the heavy workload of the farm.

The Small, Big Cat

There have been so many wonderful occasions when animals have come from spirit to aid their friends but this next case was one of the most surprising.

Janet sat in front of me, appearing quite withdrawn. She complained of neck and shoulder pain. She seemed tired and listless. She admitted that she didn't really know why she had come to see me, she had just been told by a friend that I might be able to help. She seemed quite skeptical about my methods, which was quite understandable, as even I question my sanity sometimes. However, as we lightly touched on the subject of emotional trauma, impacting on the physical systems of the body, I began to notice something very strange circling her legs. I blinked in amazement several times and struggled to make sense of this vision before me. I always ask for guidance from the universe and since Duke's appearance, was aware of the help of spirit animals, who know far more about the healing require-ments of their previous owners than me.

What I was 'seeing' was a small cat. Not some cuddly, purring, domestic puss. This was a breed of wild big cat and it was lovingly rubbing its body around my client's legs. Every so often it stared balefully at me with large penetrating eyes, which bored into me, as though to say, "Tell her!" You can imagine my dilemma. I was trying to be as delicate as possible in describing some of my more unconventional ways of working with people and here was this cat, demanding that I make its presence known.

Eventually I plucked up the courage to say that, mad as it

might seem, I could 'see' an animal 'energy' with her, that had obviously come from spirit to help her.

Janet looked rather scathingly at me, unsurprisingly, until I described what I was witnessing and she paled dramatically. She then burst into tears. I thought perhaps the cat was an Ocelot as it had wonderfully intricate patterns on its fur. But I knew this wasn't quite correct. Janet put me right. She said through her tears, "It's a Cervill".

This was an orphan that she had been given to adopt as a small child in Africa and they had become inseparable. Janet had no remnants of an Afrikaans accent, so there was no suggestion of her past home. To her amazement, the more she thought about her childhood companion, the more she was able to actually 'feel' the slight pressure around her legs as the cat lovingly rubbed in affection. She said the cat had been her constant friend, when her parents had been very absorbed in the running of their estate and the ensuing difficulties. The young Janet shared all her secrets and dreams with her feline friend, at a time when she felt confident and happy that her life would always be free, unfettered by worry. But one day her father announced that the family would have to move back to England and Janet would have to release her friend back into the wild.

She knew that the chances were minimal of the inexperienced cat surviving, and she was devastated and felt she was abandoning her charge. Janet had to leave the bewildered cat in the bush, sobbing as she had to leave the majesty of Africa's wilderness.

As she spent the rest of her life growing up in England, she often reflected on her time in Africa. She felt that she had failed her beautiful trusting friend who had relied on her for protection and all its needs.

This was a pattern we discovered had followed her throughout her adult life. Janet felt she had never really succeeded in anything. She was extremely hard on herself and

31

self-deprecating. I felt that was the cause of her neck and shoulder pain. She was literally shouldering the weight of the world on her shoulders and the pressure and tension was causing the discomfort in the neck.

The cat wanted to reassure her that it was fine in spirit and truly knew how hard Janet had tried to do her best for the cat. It only wanted Janet to forgive herself and enjoy her life from now on.

Janet seemed to change almost immediately and appeared taller and more empowered. The reassurance from the cat had started Janet's reassessment of her perceived past failures and negative self-belief. We discussed how we could re-program those memories into positive learning experiences. Thanks to a small, big cat we learnt that it was never too late to forgive ourselves and move forward in positive self-esteem.

Holly the Old English sheepdog

Wendy called me on the phone. She was very distressed and said she needed my help urgently. Poor Wendy had been through such a tough time. Her beloved Old English sheepdog Holly had been put to sleep on the operating table as her cancer had spread and the vet had thought it was the kindest thing to do. She had rung me and asked if Holly was all right with this decision. This was such a traumatic task as there was obviously so much emotion involved. Holly told me she has been ready to go, and asked me to tell Wendy to try not to be too upset, as Holly would always be around in spirit to guide her. This is all very well, but being told that and believing and gaining comfort from it are two very different things. Even though I truly believe that our animals are with us in spirit, when it comes to losing a special friend it is still devastating.

Wendy had spent several weeks grieving and was not coping well at all. Out of the blue a bitch puppy had become available and Wendy thought that perhaps if she got a new puppy it might help to ease the pain. But this was not the case. Guilt consumed her as she felt that Holly would think her disloyal and that Wendy was trying to forget her.

I arrived at Wendy's house to be met by the most gorgeous bundle of fluff. Eyes like bright, ripe, chestnuts peered out beneath curly curtains of hair. The iron-grey-and-white pup wagged her tail sheepishly and rolled on to her back, exposing her beautiful belly.

The youngster was adorable, but far from finding Wendy in raptures about her, she was distressed and still heartbroken. The pain of Holly's loss was still preying heavily on her.

The puppy had been extremely hyperactive and had experienced a mild stomach upset, which I thought was interesting, when I reflected on how stressed Wendy was. We had discussed the protein and wheat content of the puppy's diet, previously over the phone and I was glad to hear that the puppy had calmed a little.

I sat on the floor with the pup, attempting to extricate my fingers from a mouth full of needle sharp baby teeth. I thought I might have to perform a recount of my fingers. Wendy sat opposite on the sofa, trying to compose herself. I gave the pup some healing, hoping this would calm her digestion and behaviour. But I was far more concerned with Wendy. She looked drawn and exhausted. She admitted that she was seriously considering whether it had been a wise decision to get the pup.

As I listened to Wendy the most extraordinary vision began to appear next to her on the sofa. Slowly I began to distinguish the soft outline of a large hairy grey and white dog, sitting next to her. Holly began to appear, not only in front of me, but began issuing directions in my mind, as to the best way to conduct the session to facilitate the best healing for Wendy. Holly directed me to perform a healing heart visualization.

In this healing heart visualization, the person visualizes their emotional heart being repaired and filled with unconditional love – it's a very beautiful exercise with a wonderfully positive impact on releasing embedded emotions. I wondered whether it would be wise to mention the fact that Wendy had a large canine companion on the sofa next to her. Holly became adamant. She 'said' with utter conviction "Tell Wendy I am here. She must tell her heart, not to stop feeling, but to stop hurting. I know that noone could have tried harder to save me." The force of the sense of love for Wendy almost overwhelmed me and I knew if I repeated this to Wendy, it was going to be emotional.

Rather like Duke who was desperate to have his wishes made known, Holly demanded that I say the words to Wendy. I took a deep breath, wishing I had brought tissues, as I was feeling the depth of unconditional love that was filling the room. So I relayed the telepathic exchange. Wendy crumpled in tears and I surrendered to the enormity of emotion that filled us all. We were both sobbing, but this time with joy. I was filled with wonder as Holly dictated as I repeated verbatim her comforting wisdom. The puppy had curled up in my lap, only glancing in mild surprise, trying to determine what all the fuss was about. The puppy was well aware of Holly's presence ever since she had arrived at her new home. She knew exactly how Holly was feeling. It was almost as though she was saying "Oh thank goodness for that! Now we can get on with life".

Far from Holly feeling forgotten or betrayed, she was really happy that the puppy was now taking over the role of teaching Wendy what she needed to learn about herself. Holly said that Wendy was in capable hands (or paws), but that she would still be around to oversee the proceedings.

I left Wendy cuddling the puppy, with a huge smile on her face, still tearful but so grateful to Holly for her help. I had never before conducted an entire session being directed by a dog.

I reflected on the immensity of the healing that had taken place. The repaying and exchange of heartfelt love was incredible, and a huge privilege to have played a part in that exchange.

The Animals Gather to Bring Comfort to Me
On a personal note, I would like to thank all our animal companions that came forward to comfort me in my hours of need.

About a week before my mother passed away, I was lying in bed, wondering how on earth I could endure the pain of losing her. She had fought her cancer with such grace, but she was finally losing her battle. I knew that she had done her work here and needed to grow through her passing into her next phase on her soul's journey, but that knowledge did little to alleviate the sadness I was experiencing then.

Suddenly, I was being led through the pages of our old family photograph albums, where there were tattered old photographs of my mother with her beloved animal companions. There was Trixie, the puppy of questionable parentage that had grown into a marvelous, enormous, shaggy hound. She used to wait patiently at the end of the road for my mother to return from school after the days of enforced separation. It was as though they were helping me to remember and experience all the happy times my mother had enjoyed with her animal friends. One by one they seemed to come to life from the pages and gather around me in support. All the animals that had been companions in her childhood and through my own childhood appeared before me. I could see horses, ponies, dogs, cats and rabbits, from the old photographs, as though preparing a welcoming committee for her. They were all there in spirit waiting to greet her and here they were reassuring me that all would be well. Though still desperately sad, I was comforted by their presence and prayed that I would have a similar welcome when my time would come.

My mother had adored her animals and patiently welcomed all the waifs and strays I had brought home as a child, despite our lack of funds and space. I have so many memories of her stories of her escapades with her animal friends as a young child growing up in Devon. Two days before she died, I was sitting with her by her bed and I could 'see' standing next to her, her old Exmoor pony, Robin, in spirit. I could clearly see his 'mealy' muzzle, the soft biscuit colour that Exmoors are famous for, and his large doe-like eyes. He had been rather too strong for her, and I remember her anecdotes of when he had transported her rather faster than she had wished to go, on many an occasion.

Robin told me that if my mother wished, he would take her very gently, on their favourite ride. My mother thought it would be a lovely visualization. She was tired of being in her bed, tired of feeling so weak and tired of life. I suggested that she allow Robin to take her and to enjoy her ride. She closed her eyes in peaceful meditation for about thirty minutes. When she opened her eyes, she said Robin had been really good and she had had a wonderful ride all along her childhood haunts, but she was very cross to have returned to her bed. When the time came for her to pass, there was her mother, who had died when my mother was just sixteen, standing next to her, holding out her hand from spirit to guide her. My grandmother, who was my namesake, told me that she was looking after all the animals. They were all waiting to greet my mother along with much loved members of the family that had now passed to spirit. When I finally returned home on that dreadful day, I sought out Mulberry and sat with her lying next to me under a large oak tree in our field. She leaned her glossy warm body next to me soaking up my tears, comforting me in my desolation. I couldn't speak to anyone else, only Mulberry seemed to understand in her tacit consolation.

CHAPTER 3

Animal Soul Retrieval and Trauma Release

The more I was asked to work with traumatized horses, the more they intuitively showed me how to repair and re-empower them. I had heard of the concept of 'soul retrieval' in humans. Indigenous tribal shamans or healers had used these methods for centuries. The shaman 'travelled' in their minds, back in time to the event of situation that had caused so much trauma to the person they were treating. They believed the person had become fragmented, as though a part of their soul had split away and that they would never be 'whole' again. Until that part was retrieved and somehow placed back within the person's being, they would never be truly 'healed'. When the horses began to show me in my mind what they had experienced, like horrendous video clips, they instructed me how to retrieve the missing parts of their soul blueprint. These were parts that had been shattered by traumatic situations that had occurred not only in this life, but also in their past lives.

They also described how, on many occasions, they had been with their present owners, back in the past and they had reunited to heal some unresolved trauma. Again these wonderful creatures were choosing to reincarnate to help us. Mulberry had been a fine example of this, though when she was alive she never showed me her past traumas – she was far too busy helping us. Only when **we** were ready to understand her deeper connections with Cameron, did she reveal her role. Even stranger and yet another new concept for me to assimilate was that they were not always horses in their previous lives. This took some understanding, but after several cases of 'seeing' horses as zebras, mules and donkeys, I began to accept that I had to be prepared for anything.

Shannon the Horse with 100 Past Lives

The most astounding case I have ever encountered was with Shannon. She was a strong bay mare that had become extremely unpredictable. Her owner was becoming desperate as she could be quite dangerous. She was not malicious in any way, just incredibly anxious at practically everything she experienced in her life.

The horses had 'showed' me that their past self could appear behind me, a shadowy energy form like a holographic outline. This previous incarnation presence would then pass through me, using me as a vehicle, as I blew the fragmented part back into the animal. Usually they re-entered at the shoulder, but sometimes I blew the lost part into a physical area that had been damaged in the past.

This was very strange for me at first as the animal's energy passed through my mouth into the animal. I could 'see' the final parts of the animal, the hind hooves and end of the tail disappear into the living animal in front of me, I then knew that the missing 'part' had been returned.

As I approached Shannon, she was quite agitated. I could feel her assessing whether I posed as some sort of threat. Her nostrils flared and her eyes were wide. She seemed to be locked into some eternal victim mode. She began to show me that in many lifetimes she had been victim of a predator, or had been in situations where she had been helpless to escape. One of her many fears were to be shut in and she also hated any loud noises, especially of a metallic nature. There were corrugated roofs on the stables where she lived, so if these banged or rattled in the wind, she would become very distressed.

She showed me a lifetime when she had been a dray horse in London during the blitz. A bomb had fallen on the building where she had been stalled and she had been hit and mortally injured by the fragments of metal, wood and stone. The sense of helplessness and inability to escape was overwhelming. This seemed to be a repeated pattern as she showed me many lifetimes of trauma. The first of her terrible experiences was as a tiny eohippus that was attacked and killed by a creature rather like a sabre tooth tiger. I had a very clear picture of the prehistoric creature with its toes that would later evolve into hooves. The more she showed me these 'video clips' in my mind, the longer the procession of animal hologram fragments grew. I patiently allowed her to divulge as much as she was able. This took enormous courage for her and I felt hugely privileged to be trusted enough to delve into her past. Only when she was ready and gave me permission, did I commence with the re-integration of all her past selves. One by one they queued, waiting to jump into me as pure 'energy', passing through me back into Shannon. This may appear quite strange, but I have learnt to completely trust my guidance and the instructions of the animal involved, even though this has been a vertical learning curve! They have taught me to remove my doubting ego.

I don't know if there were actually a hundred past life holograms that passed through me, I lost count, but it certainly felt like it! Eventually she became calmer. She also showed the tears and dents in her aura energy field from the bomb blast, so I was guided to imagine repairing it the best way that I could.

I visualized expanding her aura and knocking out all the dents and repairing all the torn areas, somehow making her whole again. I truly hoped that this would help. I feel that the power of our healing intent is paramount and that wonderful healing **can** take place.

Shannon did become calmer, but did still have occasional unpredictable moments. I would have liked to have worked with her more as there were so many 'layers' to this horse. I reflected on her choices to have reincarnated so many times in order to experience so many traumas. I wondered why this had been the case and hoped that finally in this life she could believe that she no longer has to be a victim.

Manic Meg

I have had several cases where dogs needed this method of healing, where a holographic image of the dog could also appear to be 'returned' to its present 'self'.

Meg was brought to me as a last resort and unfortunately I don't think her owner was entirely open to my rather strange methods. I was saddened because I felt the dog was desperately trying to help its owner understand why she was behaving that way. She seemed to be constantly wide eyed and panting. I was told that she was permanently anxious, especially out on a walk and in open spaces. Of course, collies are renowned and famous for their herding instinct. It is quite common for a collie to want everyone to keep together on a walk, so they can 'guard' their flock, but her anxiety was excessive.

When I asked Meg to show me why she was so anxious, she started to run some images in my mind, it was like watching some video footage of the Second World War. Rather like Sam, the Jack Russell puppy, she started to change her appearance into that of a German shepherd dog. I witnessed a scene that was quite distressing. She showed me her present owner as an officer who was shot and she was his dog. Sadly she felt that she had failed her master, because she could not save him. As Meg returned to her normal collie appearance, I visualized returning the trauma-tized German shepherd into her.

Meg explained that she was constantly worried that her master would be hurt again. So I reassured her that this need never happen again and how wonderful it was that they were together and that she should now just enjoy her life. I didn't have any news of Meg's progress, but hoped that one day her human friend would come to realize how much she cared for him.

Conker the sensitive stallion

I was lucky enough to be asked to visit Conker, a very handsome stallion. He was sweet natured and affectionate, but became very distressed and unmanageable at the sound of loud noises. Telepathically, he 'told' me he had been shouted at when he had been at a previous stud. Far from being a tough, macho horse, he was incredibly sensitive and easily upset. Noise seemed to be the key factor with him.

I asked him to show me why he was so frightened by loud sounds. He asked me to question his owner about a little boy that he had shown me a picture of in my mind.

I described what I was visualizing and she told me that there was indeed a little boy that fitted that description who came to see Conker regularly. The owner said they seemed to have a very special relationship. Conker affirmed that he loved the little boy and that they had been together before in a past life.

He showed me a time in Wales when they worked in the coal mines, the small boy struggling in his life of toil and grime. The boy had always been kind and very gentle with Conker in a world where there was little sensitivity or sentimentality, and pit ponies and young children were forced to endure extremely harsh conditions. Conker said that one day he had heard the most terrible sound behind him in the mine. His small friend had gone back further down the shaft to get another pony. The awful sound of rumbling and crashing as the mine collapsed behind him had filled Conker with terror. The poor remaining ponies, men and children, were lost in the collapse of the shaft and Conker's life was never the same again as he mourned his young friend.

He showed me that he was smaller and stockier in that life and was black or very dark bay. He sported a grimy white star that tried to shine out on his forehead, but the white fur was usually caked with coal dust. As Conker showed me what he had looked like, the corresponding 'hologram' appeared and I 'blew' the black pony back into Conker. But this time I had a very precise place to return his fragmented part.

Because sound was such a vital factor in Conker's trauma, I was guided to blow the part back into his ear. Normally horses do not take kindly to having someone blow in their sensitive ears, so I wondered how he would respond. I mentally asked him if this was ok and if so, would he give me sign so that I would know that I wouldn't be upsetting him. It was also quite awkward for me to reach up into his ear to perform my task. Conker responded by lowering his head and practically shoving his ear over my mouth, which was a little disconcerting. I blew as gently as I could, Conker never flinching, as the energy of the black pony disappeared into Conker.

Conker was far happier after this and did not seem to be so worried by sound. He continued his loving relationships with his owner and the little boy, relishing their company.

Fear in the Womb

Another wonderful stallion also had a problem with sound. He showed me that he had been inflicted with his mother's fear whilst in the womb as she had been terrified by shouting. I was guided to visualize cradling him as a foetus in my arms, soothing and calming, so that he could release all his fear. It was a strange feeling holding the tiny horse's energetic form in my arms.

Once I intuited all the fear had left, I visualized returning the healed energy to the stallion. He had become very agitated during this session, but once the foetal energy was returned and the issue had been released, he was really calm and affectionate once more.

Yorrick the Mule

During one of my clinics a fine bay horse called Yorrick was brought for me to look at. He had become quite dangerous with traffic, especially anything coming up behind him. He had practically dived onto the bonnet of another car, which was obviously disastrous. I noticed that he had the most wonderful ears. His owner Julie said many people had commented on. They were long and expressively bendy in the most unusual way.

He was a very elegant horse, so I don't think that the ears suggested the past life incarnation that he consequently showed me. I asked him where his fear of things coming behind him came from. He showed me what looked like a scene from the gold rush in the Yukon. This time Yorrick was not an elegant well bred horse but a large brown mule. This was my first case where the horses had changed species, though still in the horse family – I was later to find out that this was not the only form they could take.

Yorrick told me that the old prospector who owned him was called Jack and said that Julie was the same person. They had been reunited now to heal their relationship.

They had been searching for gold in some rocky terrain. Being unsuccessful they were retiring to a small rough shanty town that had sprung up to meet the needs of the hoards that were trying their luck. The town was to be seen several miles away down the slopes of the mountain. They were negotiating their descent, when suddenly there was a growl and a huge mountain lion launched itself onto the rump of the mule. The panicked animal threw Jack and fell to the ground as the mountain lion ravaged the poor mule.

Jack desperately searched for his gun to try and save the mule but time was against him. His rifle was stuck in his saddle and his smaller hand gun had fallen from his holster. Eventually after scrabbling around in the dusty ground, he retrieved his weapon and fired. He managed to kill the marauding lion, but it was too late to save his poor faithful servant. The mule lay screaming, bleeding profusely; the only answer was to destroy his friend. Jack loved his old mule and they had spent many years together trying to better their meager existence with a payload of the precious metal. They had scraped a living and it seemed that the mule was his mainstay, underpinning his whole existence. Jack closed his eyes and pulled the trigger. After losing his mule, Jack's life deteriorated and he had spent his time drowning his sorrows in the shanty town.

When Julie had first seen Yorrick, she had felt an overwhelming feeling of guilt which was inexplicable to her then. Although it had not been financially sensible to buy him, she had felt compelled to have him, somehow they had to be together. She now understood her obsession to own him at all costs.

Most owners would have sold or put down such a potentially lethal horse, but Julie had to discover the reason for his behaviour. Once the mule's energy had been 'returned' to Yorrick and I visualized healing the terrible marks made by the mountain lion's claws that still 'showed' as an energy memory, Yorrick's whole expression changed.

I then helped Julie forgive herself and let go of any sadness she may have still been holding from that traumatic time. I was glad to hear later that Yorrick was now a model of safety on the road. He never displayed remnants of the old fears. I was pleased to have facilitated their healing and looked forward to hearing about happier events in their lives.

Nick and Lily

Of course, there have been many happy past lives where animals and their owners have shared long and contented times together. However when trauma has been stored at a cellular level, physically or emotionally, and is somehow triggered in the present, this is when problems occur.

One of the scariest horses that I have worked with was a horse called Lily. She was enormous. Not a gentle Shire-like giant, she was a finer boned creature but almost as large. She was very pushy with seemingly no spatial awareness of personal 'space'.

She was aggressive and possessive of her own space, but not considerate of anyone else's. When trapped in the confines of a stable I felt in real danger of being squished.

She did not appear overtly vicious, just very stressed. She cribbed and wind suck, which is the term for a horse that bites the door or some wooden partition and sucks air up through the mouth. It is thought to be a very bad habit and can cause much damage to wooden stables as the wood is chewed. It can also cause colic or digestive problems because of the amount of air that gets into the system.

This was another case where the owner, Nick, had felt compelled, despite better judgment, to purchase her. He somehow felt that he owed her a happy life, but could not understand this feeling. Although he recognized

Nick and Lilly

all her faults, he was fiercely protective of her and vehemently defended her to anyone who might criticize her. However, he did recognize that they needed help.

She was very difficult to handle and riding her had become impossible because she would rear as soon as anyone placed a foot in the stirrup iron. Having this huge black leviathan of a horse go straight up with you was not an experience that I would envy. We decided that it would be better to move her out to a field, rather than the confines of the stable. She still appeared stressed, but after a session of gentle healing, she became calmer and her demeanor improved. Nick noticed that her eyes, that had previously always had a furrowed expression, had changed. She seemed more at peace with herself.

She told me that she had suffered years of ill-fitting saddles and some inexperienced handling that had taken its toll on her back. She had also passed through many homes. The rearing was the anticipatory fear of back pain. I suggested treatment by a friend who was a wonderful equine cranial-sacral therapist and is very intuitive to past life issues.

Lily then showed me her past life connection with Nick. They had been together in America in something like a pony express scenario. A rattle snake had spooked Lily and they had tumbled over a ravine and sadly Lily's back had been broken. Nick confessed his horror and severe phobia of snakes when I described what Lily was showing me. This made sense when we discovered what had triggered Lily's fright. Nick had never previously been able to understand why he was so adverse to snakes.

I performed a soul retrieval for Lily and looked forward to hearing feedback of her progress from Nick. He was such a wonderful owner. I commended him for his deep love and compassion for Lily, as many other people would not have had either the patience or the commitment. She was a wonderful horse but extremely challenging.

In the interim of Lily's recuperation, Nick felt that he might need some past life healing himself. So we arranged a session where I might facilitate a release of the trauma still held within him. This seemed to help Nick on a personal level and he was far more accepting of himself after releasing the inexplicable guilt.

A few weeks later he contacted me to say that Lily was a changed animal. She was gentle and calm, so settled and affectionate. Her back had been treated and all seemed well and set to re-commence riding her.

Nick had understandably been quite frightened by her previous behavior when attempting to mount, so I suggested some positive visualization techniques. I suggested that he visualize all the lovely routes that their hacks would take them. I told him to 'see' them having a wonderful time, enjoying the Cornish countryside and beaches and returning home happy and fulfilled. I think Nick thought I was slightly deranged, but he promised that he would give it a try. He rang me a week later to ask if I could tune into Lily to see if she was ready for a ride on the following day.

Nick had worked hard with his visualizations and decided that it was now or never. I got the impression that Lily was really happy with the idea, but braced myself to hear how they had fared. That evening I received a jubilant phone call from Nick saying that Lily had been perfectly behaved and seemed to recognize the new routes as though she knew exactly where the bridal paths were taking her. I told Nick that of course she knew the routes because he had been telepathically showing her all the previous week. Nick was so pleased with their progress that he wrote to a local newspaper that ran an article on her.

Lily told me many things about her past that Nick could not verify as he knew nothing of her history. One of the events Lily described to me was that she had had a foal and felt great sadness at the separation when it was weaned.

From the photographs in the newspaper, a previous owner recognized Lily and contacted the paper, verifying everything she had been brave enough to reveal to me. The latest news from Nick was that another of his mares had foaled and Lily had looked so longingly at the foal that she was now being allowed to have another one herself. He has promised to send some photos of the foal.

Rosie the Roman Horse

Another very traumatic case was that of Rosie. She was a stunning bright bay mare, but she was in deep trouble. She had been hours away from being sent to slaughter as she had become so unmanageable, when my horse loving friend said that she would pay the owner the amount she would have fetched for meat and rescued her.

Her symptoms were that she detested being touched around her middle and girth area, especially if anyone bent down near her. So shoeing her was a nightmare. When mounting was attempted, she would spin like a Dervish and she was generally dismissed as a 'nutter'.

Rosie had arrived at my friend's stable yard wild eyed and traumatized. Her behaviour was so challenging that my friend wondered at the wisdom of her actions. Poor Rosie was in a very bad state, through her wild expression she was clearly crying out for help.

When I first saw her, Rosie seemed to distrust everyone, except my friend who she had begun to believe was trying to help her.

When I examined Rosie's energy field I intuited the traumatic memory manifesting as a sword that had impaled her from the girth line of her belly, deep into her chest. This was just about where the stirrup would hang and so any invasion into that space with someone trying to mount her would be deemed as a terrible threat. Likewise with shoeing, when the Farrier bent to lift her front leg, the memory of being stuck with the sword would have terrified her. The sword looked of Roman origin to me, so I visualized removing the sword very gently and slowly, and transmuted the energy by sending it to the light.

I imagined it turning into the most beautiful silver staff so transforming a negative image into a positive one. I then worked to send healing energy to pack the wound. Rosie had shown me the 'video clip' of her experiences so I performed a soul retrieval. She seemed immediately calmer and more accepting of our help.

Although her behavior was greatly improved and she actually enjoyed being ridden, once mounted, she was still very difficult to shoe. It was a great credit to her Farrier's patience that she was ever shod at all. I was called to see her again, to see if I could help finally release her trauma and calm her inner demons.

The poor horse showed me another life in the American Civil War when she had been killed, again with a sword, whilst being tethered in cavalry ranks. Soldiers from the opposing side had infiltrated the camp and had stealthily tried to kill the horses. Some of the horses had managed to escape, breaking their tethers, but Rosie had met her fate in terror. This explained why she seemed to have a horror of being tied up and she would stand shaking and cringing. She told me that her cavalry officer at that time was the man who had previously owned her in this life. Sadly she had found her way back to him but he was not open to being healed or healing her, so he had given up on her. He was not open to the concept of reincarnation and past life trauma. Luckily she found her way to my friend, so that we could all learn from her terrible past. I removed the second sword memory and she is now a safe ride and a well-balanced, happy horse.

How much is That Puppy in the Window?

Some believe that time is an illusion and that there is no such thing as past lives, just parallel existences, playing out different life lessons, where we choose to incarnate in different forms experientially. I don't believe that it matters whether this is true or not, I believe that all that matters is that we evolve on our soul journey and raise our vibrational energy to help raise awareness and the consciousness of the planet. I feel the biggest detriment to the planet is negative fear energy that pollutes the purity of healing Love that should encapsulate the planet and all of humanity. Animals seem aware of this and their biggest task is to reform mankind. Humans seem expert at negative thoughts and fall easily into glass being 'half empty' brigade. We have so much to learn and so much self-limiting fear to let go of. Only when we are ready to fully integrate all the pieces of our soul's evolutionary jigsaw puzzle, do our animals find us for mutual healing. Sadly this was not the case with Rosie, but perhaps next time around her previous owner will be ready to be karmically healed and she may have touched him on some deeper levels.

I feel that it is quite incredible that animals take such a journey of different homes and traumas in order to somehow contrive to return to their previous owners. Many rescue animals are finally found by their past life owners, after years in their present incarnation. I feel that we are all on a journey of self discovery.

Sometimes this reunion happens when we are 'chosen' by a particular kitten that was the only one in a litter that looked at us in that special way or clambered into our lap, or the puppy that just happened to be the last one left.

One of my dogs that I had the deepest connection with, many years ago, called to me from a pet shop window in the depths of Willesden in London. I walked past her every morning for a week as I rushed to catch my bus. She looked so mournful in her cage. She was a collie cross and like me I felt that she hated being in the confines of the city and longed to be in the country. One morning I passed the shop and she had gone. I wondered who might have bought her and wished it could have been me, as I had an inexplicable longing to have her. I had mentioned her to my boyfriend at that time and as it was my birthday he had secretly bought her for me. Imagine my surprise when my boyfriend announced that he couldn't come to see me that evening because his new girlfriend was biting his foot! He quickly explained who she was and I rushed over to collect her. Because of her I left my brief sojourn of city life and returned to the countryside, where we had seventeen happy years together.

I feel that she has returned as the rescue dog I have now.

CHAPTER 4

War wounds

Woody and Badger

Woody, the large skewbald hunter, snorted as I approached his stable. My good friend Jenny struggled to hold on to the end of his halter rope. He was becoming very agitated. He was a very handsome horse with wonderful, striking markings. Jenny had called me because this normally safe and reliable horse had suddenly become lethal. He had inexplicably started to leap off grass verges while out exercising, onto the path of any unsuspecting vehicle – alarmingly, usually a large lorry.

All he would 'say' to me was "I walked in badger's blood....I walked in badger's blood..." This was quite disconcerting, as you can imagine. I didn't understand what he was saying. I asked Jenny if she could remember riding near a dead badger, but she couldn't recall any accident or road kill. Apparently he had very nearly caused serious injury to Jenny's daughter and to himself, as he had bolted out when hunting, crashing through trees and fences. Fearing for her safety, she had baled out and he had finally been caught, and they had called me in their attempt to calm him.

With some trepidation I entered his stable. I was drawn to remove some negative energy from his front hooves as there was obviously some trapped emotion there. I will describe the healing techniques in more detail later in the chapter on negative energies and entities. I lifted each hoof and using my pendulum I visualized 'drawing' out the bad energy. I then cleansed my crystal pendulum in water. The pendulum had swung violently whilst being held over the sole of the hoof. Woody had obviously been affected by something in his feet. The only trigger Jenny could think of was that when he had recently been reshod, the Farrier had had to reposition one of the nails, leaving a tiny hole in the wall of the hoof. This is something normally very inconsequential. I asked Jenny if the challenging behavior had started before or after the shoeing and she felt that it was just after he had been shod.

After checking that the pendulum no longer showed any 'negative energy', I tried to check on the rest of Woody's body, but he was having none of it! Both Jenny and I felt that discretion was the better part of valour and we removed ourselves from his stable. He was really anxious now. As I closed the stable door and was sliding the bolt, he dropped two words into my head that made my blood run cold, "The Somme".

Woody

This was obviously referring to an excruciatingly painful past life experience that he was clearly in no fit condition to divulge any further information about. I tried to reassure him and telepathically told him that he could 'talk' to me any time he felt able and I would do my best to help him release some of the trauma, but that I quite understood that he was unable to think about it at present. I was deeply troubled by Woody's pain and wished that I could have helped more. I hoped that he might feel able to let me help him at some time. Like working with humans, animals have to dictate the pace of emotional of physical release. Only when they are ready, can progress be made.

I was awakened the small hours of the morning at 3am to find Woody almost screaming at me in my head, that he wanted to tell me the story of what had happened in that dreadful battle of a terrible war. He ran a video clip of the horrific events.

He 'showed' me himself as a bay horse, with his best friend

who was black with a large white blaze. This horse was called Badger. The conditions were appalling. The death and destruction of life was disturbing to witness. The foul mud seemed to claw and consume everything. Badger took a direct hit from mortar fire and the gore and carnage that ensued were unspeakable. Woody was injured and fell in the mud. He was dragged to his feet by his panicked soldier and was forced to stagger through the remains of his best friend.

As this was the first occasion I had been 'shown' such horrendous information remotely, I was unsure of how to proceed and whether it might be some bizarre and sick dream. But I knew that I was awake, I knew how sick I felt and the extent of the horror and despair that Woody was 'showing' me. I tried my best to reassure Woody that I would help as best I could and I would come to see him again as soon as possible. At that time I had not attempted to perform distant soul retrievals.

At a more sociable hour I rang Jenny and asked if I could visit Woody again and I told her what had transpired. We felt that Woody must have walked on some remnants of a road kill. Maybe the tiny hole in his hoof after being reshod had allowed the energy of the animal that had been killed on the road to permeate somehow that shock had been the trigger to bring all this past life horror to the fore.

When I arrived at Jenny's farm I entered the large barn that stabled several of her hunt hire horses and her husband Tony's point-to-pointers. There was Woody's lovely bright head straining out to meet me. This time he seemed far more receptive and ready to work on his trauma. I mentally visualized the horrific scene and brought back the energetic imprint of the bay horse that had been Woody, visualizing him as whole and healed, with no injuries, as he gently passed back into Woody. He allowed me to perform this quite readily, but was still devastated about the welfare of Badger.

Strange as it may seem, I called upon the skills of Troy, our old horse. I was guided to remotely 'ask' him to bring back Badger from spirit to prove to Woody that his friend had been healed in spirit. Somehow they had never re-connected after Woody's death and they had both remained 'locked' in their state of trauma.

Troy had helped me before with a very angry pony which was still carrying immense trauma from leaving its mother, even though the pony was now quite old. He made the most frightening, biting lunges at anyone that dared enter his loose box. His dam had naturally died by then. I mentally pictured Troy in his field at home and 'asked' him to help. Miraculously, Troy somehow managed to bring the 'spirit energy' of the pony's mother back to calm him. I could make out the tenuous faint vision of a mare behind the pony. What was more astounding was that the pony turned to look at the vision obviously very aware of its presence and immediately became calm.

I had heard that since then the pony still made rather rude faces at people, but was generally much happier and friendlier. I hoped that the same tactics would prove as successful with Woody. Troy was becoming an important healing ally. This special horse proved to possess even more amazing healing talent later.

I mentally asked for Troy's help and very slowly a shadowy vision appeared behind Woody. I could just distinguish the dark form of Badger's head and his pale blaze.

To my great pleasure Woody turned, his eyes as if on stalks, and stared at his old friend. If spirit animals could return to help their human counterparts, I saw no reason why this should not occur with animals as well. It was amazing to witness Woody's expression of surprise and relief as he 'saw' that Badger was fine and that all was well.

He could now progress with his emotional healing and finally release the entire past trauma. The only problem was that Woody told me his old friend didn't much care for the confines of a stable and that they were rather cramped. So Woody was moved to an open barn with other horses, so there would be plenty of room for Woody to socialize with his old friend from spirit any time he felt like 'dropping' in. I am pleased to hear from Jenny that Woody is now back to his old safe self and enjoying life.

War Horses

After Woody's case, these harrowing war past lives with horses started to surface from all directions. I asked my guides why I was being shown such horrific cases as if they were coming out of the woodwork.

I was 'told' that horses hold the war consciousness for man. I asked for more clarity on that statement. Thanks to the horses' tutelage, I was now called to help release this and help all the damaged animals that had been forced by man to participate in our conflicts with our fellow man. Such a terrible price has been paid, not only by the animals and man, but also the planet that has been desecrated. For us as a race, this abomination has to be healed. It seems that many horses are choosing to help us understand the negative force of our actions and help transmute this war consciousness.

I reflected on the level of compassion and the depth of love that the horses must have, to be willing to carry that burden. It almost made me ashamed to be human when I thought about man's senseless destruction over millennia. If I can be used as a tool to play a small part in aiding the healing of the planet's pain, then I will be fulfilling my role in this lifetime. By raising awareness of the horses' role and doing my best to help them release their trauma and somehow educate people, I hope that I am achieving my life's purpose.

Poppet, Wynn and Solomon

Poppet was a dark bay mare with a fantastic talent for show jumping. I was working with other horses on her yard, when Nadia, her owner asked me to have a 'chat' with her.

I immediately felt that there was a real problem with Poppet's head. Nadia told me that the mare was extremely sensitive with her bridle and the horse showed me several different bits that had been fitted without success. Her mouth was incredibly sensitive so it was extremely important that the correct bit be fitted. When Poppet 'showed' me the reason for this extreme sensitivity, I was not surprised at Nadia's challenges.

Poppet showed me nightmarish images and my guides told me that she had been involved in a battle at Ypres, in the First World War. Her lovely head had been smashed by an explosion and she had died a gruesome death. I visualized repairing her head in the way that a sculptor reconstructs a head from the information of a skull. This might sound strange, but I just performed the tasks that I was guided to do.

Her lovely eyes shone out at me and I asked her permission to retrieve her missing, traumatized part. Like Conker, she lowered her head and allowed me to 'blow' back her reconstructed old self. She had a very important competition the following day so I hoped that she would enjoy herself. I felt that Poppet took pride in her talent and if she could overcome some of her anxieties she would enjoy her success.

Some horses really do not want to race or jump or fulfill whatever demands we choose to inflict on them. But others really enjoy feeling the excitement and the atmosphere of the hunt or the race. I hope that I can help 'marry' those talents between horse and rider so that they can deepen their love and trust of each other, to reach their true potentials, on what ever level that might be. Whether it is the Grand National, a happy hack or just being companions, the special relationship with these animals is so important to us. If the only way most people can connect with their animals, is by imposing **their** will, then I feel it is my job to help that partnership be as harmonious and happy as possible. When owners realize just how much their animal knows and cares about them, they often begin to realize the far deeper connotations of their relationship.

When performing a distant reading for a client called Kasia on her horse Solomon, I discovered that he too, had been at Ypres in that dreadful battle. What was amazing was that just before my intuitive reading, she had had a terrible nightmare. She dreamt that she had run out into the night as she felt something terrible had happened to Solomon. He had been shot, she also had some injury, but she was devastated at not being able to save him. She had woken from this dream understandably distressed. She soon received my reading which explained the reason for the dream state bringing this past life trauma to the surface of her consciousness. I knew nothing of her dream at the time, but I intuited that they had both been in the Great War and had struggled in the desperate fight in France. Solomon was a gun horse pulling the heavy artillery which Kasia as a soldier was responsible for. The soldier loved Solomon and was terrified at their plight. So many brave young men and beautiful horses had perished, and their orders, which had to be obeyed, seemed futile and pointless. The gun carriage had got bogged down in the mud and the soldier was struggling to help the horse pull the gun free. Suddenly they were hit by enemy fire. The soldier was hit in the shoulder, but Solomon took the brunt of the spray of bullets, certainly saving the soldier's life. Sadly the horse succumbed to his wounds. The soldier somehow survived, but was heartbroken and never again felt any joy in his life. His traumas left not only physical wounds, but permanent emotional shock. He was invalided out of the war but the toll was too great.

I felt that they had been reunited to heal all that sadness and trauma at last.

I asked Kasia how she had felt when she first saw Solomon. She said that she had felt absolutely compelled to buy him, that no matter what, they had to be together. He had several physical 'faults' which logic dictated would not be sensible to purchase this horse, but she dismissed her concerns and bought him anyway. They were very happy but there always seemed to be some inexplicable, nagging fear in the back of Kasia's mind that something awful might happen to Solomon. Once the reason for this fear was released and the understanding of the past life trauma was explained, they both could let go of the past and firmly enjoy their future together.

It was amazing that Kasia should have experienced the dream just before receiving the reading. I felt that perhaps Solomon was preparing her for the reading, so that she should fully receive the healing that would take place and appreciate just how deep their relationship was.

I am always amazed at how we are destined to meet again on our soul journeys to resolve and heal ourselves. The universe contrives to allow us to grow through our life experiences on our collective soul journeys.

Wynn was another horse that was involved in the war but this time she told me she was at Flanders. She had been displaying physical problems with her hocks and had battled with intermittent lameness. She had been x-rayed and treated conventionally without lasting success, so whilst I was working on another horse, Wynn's owner asked me to have a look at her to see if I could help. I was shocked to be 'shown' her lovely dapple grey quarters and hind legs peppered with shrapnel wounds. Using my pendulum, I visualized removing the negative energy. Then I mentally removed the offending metal fragments of the past life trauma that were 'energetically' still stuck in the tissue's cellular memory. I'm sure her owner wondered what on earth I was doing, pulling imaginary objects out of her horse's backside! Fortunately she could not see what I was intuiting as it was not a pretty sight. It is always imperative to transmute negative energy into positive images. So I visualized the metal fragments turning into beautiful white butterflies that floated away removing the trauma forever. This may sound very bizarre but I just followed my guidance and the feedback from Wynn's owner was most encouraging. Her soundness issues were greatly improved and I was hopeful of a full recovery.

Cracker

Cracker was a beautiful bright bay mare that was plagued by the most awful sarcoids. These ugly large wart-like eruptions in the skin of a horse are notoriously difficult to treat and can cause real discomfort if they grow in places on the body that might be affected by tack or harness. This poor mare was covered in these horrible lumps under her belly, between her hind legs high up and into her teats. As her legs rubbed together, the sarcoids became inflamed and bloody, causing great discomfort and worry from flies. They had been treated with some potent caustic ointment, but had then reappeared more numerous than ever. Her owner Joan asked if I could help.

Again I was shown a terrible battle, this time in the Napoleonic War. Cracker showed me her present owner as an officer in a very distinctive uniform, showing in great detail the colours and braid on the tunic and the plumed helmet. They had both been hit by cannon fire and the present sarcoids seemed to have manifested as a remnant of the injuries she had sustained from the flying hot metal. I saw the force of the explosion lift her from the ground, blasting the horse's belly, and hitting her rider all down the right side. Joan told me that indeed she suffered strange aches and pains in the right side of her body.

I worked to help Cracker by visualizing tying gold cable ties around each sarcoid, to cut off the trauma energy. I also gave healing to Joan. As with Wynn, I had to treat energetic wounds from pieces of metal that were locked in her soul memory and were manifesting as physical conditions in the present. Despite my best efforts, I don't feel that Joan approved of my strange method of working with wounds from past lives, so I never heard if it helped. I truly hope that Cracker felt some relief as her prognosis was not good.

Chester the Brave heart

Jane asked me to visit her lovely chestnut Chester. Judith, her holistic vet (the same vet who had advised me with my goat Mulberry) had felt that they needed my help. I had worked on several of Judith's ponies ascertaining their past life traumas and she intuitively felt that Chester was another candidate for some soul retrieval work.

Chester showed me that he had been involved in a battle rather like a scene from a battle between the Scots and the tyrannical English. The Scots had resorted to using lethal long wooden stakes to combat the onslaught of the heavy horse regiments that the English utilized to crush the marauding Scots. They had previously had no defense against the charges, but by employing the use of stakes they incurred terrible damage to the horses and their soldier riders. Poor Chester had been impaled by one of these stakes and I had to visualize removing the offending stake and packing the wound with healing energy.

Under his chest, in the midst of a totally pure block of chestnut colour, he had a circular patch of white hair, which was at the same point as the entry site of the stake in his past life. Jane had been suffering from recurring back pain for many years, and when we had a session together, there was a similar injury deep in her lower back. I performed the same techniques and Jane's backache disappeared. There are many cases, where the underlying cause of physical pain, strange symptoms or psychological anxieties, panic or fears is traced during a past life recall, when recovery is dramatic after a healing. Chester and Jane are progressing well, working through their challenges – one of which is a fear of tractors with silage spikes, which is quite understandable under the circumstances. Once again a horse had found its way back to its previous owner to resolve their shared trauma and I marveled at the level of commitment these creatures have.

Since treating Jane and Chester, I have worked with several similar cases of horses that have been impaled by a stake. A beautiful mare that was full of anxieties had large whorls of fur on exact corresponding sides of the neck and she showed me a past life when a stake had penetrated right through her neck and she had reincarnated carrying the trauma that had manifested as a very highly strung nature with this curious hair growth. After removing the trauma, she was a much calmer animal. Her whole energy changed so much that her posture changed and her back altered so dramatically that her saddle that had just been fitted, no longer fitted her correctly and had to be readjusted!

Apex the Crying Horse

The most emotional and personally humbling case I have ever experienced was with Apex. He is what you might politely describe as a bit of a character. He had terrorized several grooms and farriers and was treated with a healthy respect in his livery yard. He was deeply loved by his owner, who had called me in to look at her dressage horse. After great success with that horse, she asked me to have a look at Apex.

She had warned me that he could be difficult. I felt that other members of the yard were speculating as to how I would fare with this large horse with an explosive personality.

Luckily for me he was an absolute lamb. I felt that he commanded the utmost respect and deserved to be treated with great humility. I slowly **Apex** approached his stable trying to convey my honest desire to help him and sending a connection of deep love from my heart to his. He responded by fixing me with a very discerning gaze, as I waited for him to allow me to enter his domain. He permitted me to enter, then allowed me to work up through his whole body, releasing tensions and balancing his physiological and emotional systems. I was then drawn to stand in front of his head, which he lowered, then he placed his muzzle in my cupped hands. He then proceeded to permeate my mind with yet another disturbing war torn scene. I began to feel choked with emotion, which I knew were his feelings that were trapped inside him. But far from being some past life event, I discovered that this poor horse had endured horrendous emotional pain in **this** lifetime. He showed me stark concrete buildings, intense heat and very arid ground, and several horses all fleeing in terror. One grey mare in particular seemed very important to Apex and I could feel his fear for her welfare. The sound of machine guns rattled through my brain. I saw bullets ricocheting off the walls of the concrete structures and fragments flying as the bullets hammered the walls. I knew Apex was telling me the account of what had happened so that I would understand how he was feeling and the extent of his underlying anger. The lovely grey mare was shot and killed, as were several others, and I felt Apex's despair. He seemed to be carrying enormous guilt that he had not been able to protect her and dismay at why he had survived where others had perished.

I relayed everything that I was being shown by Apex to his owner. I had to admit I was a little confused as this seemed a very real and present event. She then told me his history which made perfect sense of his revelations. Apparently he had been one of many horses owned by English people in Kuwait. There had been about a hundred horses kept in a large equitation centre. When war abruptly broke out, the people were forced to flee the country, leaving their horses to fend for themselves, much to the chagrin of their owners. When the conflict was finally quelled, the owners returned to attempt to rescue their horses. Sadly only very few had survived.

His previous owner had found Apex in a very sad state,

emotionally and physically. As his present owner was confirming everything that he was showing me, the emotion that was coming from Apex was totally overwhelming, as I struggled to fight back my tears. As we had progressed through the session the most extraordinary thing happened. Apex's head had become heavier and heavier in my hands as he surrendered his emotions. Suddenly both his eyes started to discharge clear fluid that poured down his cheeks. I had discovered that sometimes horses can release clear fluid from the nostrils when releasing emotions, but this was incredible. His owner said "He's crying!" Tears streamed down his face. I was filled with awe at how this horse, which had carried so much grief, guilt and anger at the perpetrators of his friend's demise, had still managed to function at all. When it seemed that he had released his tears, he started to give the most enormous yawns, which is a really good sign of recovery and release of trauma. After that, he seemed to have a completely different facial expression; it seemed lighter and less care-worn. His eyes seemed brighter somehow. He gave a big snort and I was dismissed.

There have been many times when I have felt utterly privileged to be trusted enough to help an animal, but being allowed to help Apex was one of the greatest.

CHAPTER 5

Negative Energies and Entities

Sometimes, when working with humans and animals, rather unpleasant energies make their presence felt and the more sensitive you become, the more aware you must be that these energies exist and can affect us. We need to make sure that we have a good system of protection to prevent these energies latching on to us, or draining us of our positive energy. When working with students, I recommend imagining special cloaks of protection that can wrap us safely or surrounding ourselves in white light. This can be a very personal thing and it is important to work with whatever feels right for the individual. My power animals and guides work to protect me, but protection is an important consideration when working with less positive aspects of this work.

Neville and Graham

I was summoned by Denise to see her young skewbald yearling Neville. When I arrived he was prancing around his paddock, looking very full of himself and he had a lot to say!

Denise had told me that Neville had formerly been the epitome of gentleness and loved to cuddle with her husband Graham, but recently they had been forced to quit their cuddly relationship, as inexplicably Neville attempted to attack Graham at any oppor- tunity. He had become extremely dangerous and Graham, who was so kind to all the horses, couldn't understand what had got into the young horse. Graham was upset and they had seriously considered selling their lovely horse, but desperately wanted to find out the reason for his drastic personality change. A friend had mentioned that I worked in some rather strange ways and might be able to 'talk' to Neville and extract an explanation.

As I drew closer to the electric fence that partitioned the field, I was bombarded with a very disconcerting message from Neville. "It's the black man, it's the black man."

I didn't know what to make of this and being a little concerned about sounding racist and not wanting to give offence, I delicately asked Denise if this might mean anything to her.

Their blank expressions gave my answer. So telepathically I pleaded with Neville to give me more information, as I was at a loss to understand what on earth he was trying to say. It was almost as if he 'tut-tutted' at me at my stupidity and then he said, "Ask them about Graham's new job and his left leg."

At the risk of sounding completely demented, I conveyed Neville's pearls of wisdom. I mentioned that Neville had said that I needed to ask about the new job and wondered if Graham was experiencing any strange feelings in his left leg. Neville then

showed me a picture of Graham painting skirting boards. I really felt that I needed to doubt my sanity by this time. But I knew that Neville was adamant that I repeated his communications with me. Denise looked a little surprised, but Graham went decidedly pale. He blurted out that he had indeed started a new job recently, yes he was experiencing strange pains and tingles in his left leg and he had been painting skirting boards at his place of work. So what on earth

Neville and Graham

had this to do with Neville's savage attacks? Neville was becoming frustrated by now and was 'shouting' in my head "Ask him about the job!" Neville then showed me a young boy of about ten or eleven who was very troubled and had obviously been abused by a dark skinned man. This was again like a video clip in my head.

When I questioned Graham further in order to satisfy Neville's nagging tone, he described how he had started work quite recently in a youth hostel and he had been doing some work in the bedrooms, painting the skirting boards whilst kneeling on the floor. He thought back and realized the strange feeling in his leg had commenced around this time, and admitted that this was when Neville's attacks had also begun. He said that they often had respite care children staying at the hostel, to enjoy some country air and build their confidence and self–esteem. There had been some boys of that age that Graham had noticed and they were staying in the dormitory that he had been painting.

What Neville retorted next was really quite bizarre. He explained that Graham had somehow picked up a negative entity from the boy that was carrying trauma from his abuser, who was obviously a very negative person. It was rather like a black cloud that seemed to attach itself and claw at the energy field of the boy. As the boy gained confidence and felt happier in himself, the energy loosened its grip, and as Graham was a kind positive person he somehow contracted this horrible black cloud that attached itself to Graham's leg. I agree that this may sound very far-fetched, but Neville explained that he wasn't trying to attack Graham; he was trying to attack the negative energy and remove it from his human friend. A rather dazed Graham permitted me to grovel around on the ground around his leg. I apologized as it seemed that the whole session which was supposed to be about Neville, had turned its focus towards Graham, who was not really au fait with all this 'psychic stuff'. But he took it in good heart and said he didn't mind what I did as long as he could have his old loving relationship back with Neville.

I was guided to remove the black cloud energy with my pendulum. I visualized the pendulum, as it swung around, drawing out all the energy and wrapping itself around the pendulum. I then cleansed the pendulum in water. I asked

Graham how his leg was feeling and to his amazement all the tingling had gone. I imagined wrapping Graham in a bubble of white light to protect him and restore any 'energy drain'. I also felt that this might help Neville accept him again and reassure him that the nasty black cloud had gone for good. I was a little concerned at how Neville would behave the next time Graham dared to go into his paddock, but Neville reassured me that he only had his human companion's well being at heart. I was gratified to hear that the next day Graham went in with Neville and he was back to his old self thoroughly enjoying their cuddles once more.

The concept of negative energies and entities is a belief system that ancient Shamans and healers have intuited for thousands of years. Some of the more negative uses of ancient methods can utilize these negative intents and energies. Psychic attack is well known in the field of intuitives. This may take the form of just feeling drained by someone who saps your energy or feeling really ill, literally by someone's 'ill will'. Shamans would use a rattle to drive out the energy and I have an old flame tree seed pod that I use sometimes to rattle a person's energy field, to intuit where there may be blockages of energy and negative energies may be attached.

It's amazing how many energies attach themselves to people who may know someone who can clear them. In the case of spirit energies they can very often latch onto people who then ask me to release them to the light. This may be difficult to comprehend, but I can only say that the animals have shown me so many cases of this, that I have come to understand the implications of how intensely animals feel these energies.

Dudley the Dog Causes Trouble

A prime case of an animal becoming intensely distressed by spirit and negative energies was Dudley, the wheaten terrier. His poor owner had rung me having been driven almost to distraction by the disturbing and aggravating behaviour of her dog. When I arrived at the house I was greeted by a biscuit-coloured whirlwind. He frantically raced around the house, barking and throwing himself at any light reflections; the French doors that had to be kept open or Dudley would really 'lose the plot' in his over-excitement. He was also very distracted by an area in the back garden of the house where he would throw himself and bark at apparently absolutely nothing. He seemed to be in a permanent state of anxiety and never seemed to be able to relax and switch off from his manic vigil. This made quiet evenings in front of an idyllic open log fire in their beautiful home, very tense, as Dudley would suddenly launch an attack at thin air and disrupt their peace.

They adored him, but his behaviour was really getting them down. He was a lovely dog and on the rare occasions when he would remain still long enough for me to 'feel' his energy and attempt to 'chat' with him, I felt he had a wonderful temperament. I knew that he was not happy and was quite exhausted by his constant exertion. He had been seen by an animal behaviorist, who had made some very useful suggestions, but it still remained a puzzle as to what he was 'seeing' that needed so much attention. When we went into the garden, Dudley became extremely agitated and rushed at the corner of the garden where there were some old sheds and log pile. He kept showing me pictures of bones. But these bones did not fill him with pleasure, as most dogs would be, he was feeling real fear. I got the impression that a lot of animals had met their death there and Dudley, being a sensitive little chap, was really picking up on it. When I mentioned this as tactfully as I could to his owner, she said that indeed this area of the house had originally been a butcher's and they would have killed and hung a lot of animals out the back of the shop in the old days. Not only was Dudley being plagued by all the animals spirits outside – there were human spirits inside and negative energy lines, running alongside where the French doors opened out into the garden. No wonder this dog was a nervous wreck!

Using my pendulum I 'cleared' the energy lines and intuited that some former owners of the house became quite upset when so much of their old house had been refurbished and altered structurally. This house was very old and had gained many additions over the years and was much altered from its original form. This spirit activity is very common in old houses which have been renovated and the spirit-entity of previous occupants disapproves of what the current owners have done to **their** house.

I visualized creating a pillar of light and invited the spirits to go to the light where they might be healed and free from mundane earthly worries. There was suddenly a mass exodus and Dudley, though a little confused, seemed to calm a little. I suggested to Dudley's owner that she contact a homeopathic vet and get some remedies that would help calm him and perhaps make him a little less oversensitive. On my return home I employed the help of Dave my shaman friend and we released the animal spirits that were trapped in the back garden. This took sometime as there were so many.

That dear little dog was trying so hard to alert his owners to the spirit energies trapped there. He was trying to protect his owners from any negative affects this might have had.

Although Dudley still barks at reflections, I am glad to say that he is much happier and even snuggles down with his lovely owners in front of the fire and together, they can actually manage to have a quiet, relaxing, night in.

Parker's Green 'Slime'

Parker was a magnificent thoroughbred racehorse that had come to Jenny and Tony's farm, where Woody lived. Tony wanted to train him to run in Point to Point races. The only trouble was that he never managed to relax and enjoy his grazing in the rolling

Devon countryside, as all the other horses seemed to hate and detest him. They would attempt to attack him at every available opportunity. Poor Parker was losing condition and looking miserable, isolating himself at the far end of his huge field to escape the attention of the other horses. He had to 'dice with death' as he dodged flashing teeth and hooves when he was led out of the field for me to see him. It was far too unsafe to work with him in the field. Naturally he was rather stressed as he charged through the gateway and stood snorting and shaking in front of me. Tony was hanging on for 'grim death', to his halter rope, as he extricated Parker from the attacks. As I looked closer at the horse's energy field, I was amazed to 'see' intuitively that he had a negative sort of green slimy force field around him and another black cloud energy that lingered over him. This was quite a shock and I wondered what on earth I was being shown.

I was guided to imagine a white light pouring down onto the offending cloud and transmute it into shining light. I then visualized peeling off the slime and allowing the white light to purify it. This all seemed very strange at the time, but I could only accept that I had to act on my guidance. Parker told me that he had somehow contracted this 'black cloud' energy from another horse from a yard where they were not sympathetically cared for. Ever since then he had felt depressed and every other horse that came into contact him seemed to treat him like some kind of Jonah. The green slime seemed to have resulted from a conglomeration of all the negative feelings that had been directed at Parker. I questioned myself as to whether I should divulge this information to Jenny and Tony at the risk of sounding completely mad. But fortunately they are extremely open-minded and caring of their animals. The horses work hard in their care but they make every effort to ensure they are as happy emotionally and physically as possible. They were quite intrigued with Parker's revelation and obviously the proof of whether I had managed to be effective with clearing this problem was when he was turned back out with his field mates. I tried to surround him with as much positivity and light as possible, visualizing him literally shining in positive energy.

We braced ourselves and I took a deep breath as Tony led Parker through the gate to his waiting 'welcoming committee'. Parker immediately started to race to the far end of the field, automatically distancing himself from his former attackers, but as there was no ensuing attack of any kind, he hesitated and turned to look at the others. A large bay mare who had been one of the most vicious perpetrators, ambled up to him, looking puzzled. She sniffed and seemed to be assessing his new 'energy'. The other onlookers watched to see what this dominant mare would do next. To our amazement she just tossed her head and turned away and started to graze. Even Parker looked surprised at their disinterest, so he tentatively started to graze near them. I felt a great sense of relief and thanks coming from him. I was so glad to have helped and very grateful for my guidance which I was learning to trust, however bizarre the methods seemed to be.

Chippy

Chippy was an extremely proud black and white cat. He lived with a lovely family in a beautiful house in the Blackdown Hills, an area of outstanding natural beauty in Somerset. I was called to have a chat with him as he had been displaying some very challenging behavior that was putting his future at this beautiful home at risk. Apparently, rather like Neville the horse, he had always been very affectionate with their daughter Cara, but had taken to biting her when she returned from school. Cara was devoted to Chippy and her mother was becoming worried as she

Chippy

dreaded how Chippy would react when Cara came home. Needless to say Cara was also anxious.

I ascertained from Chippy that he was indeed very regal and felt that everyone in the house were his 'subjects'. He had been horrified at his neutering experience and was holding substantial anger from his treatment.

His demeanor reminded me of my own cat Zappa, who would give me a very similar withering look. After years of him being a rather brusque character, he deigned to climb on my bed one day and I decided to question him. I asked Zappa why he always seemed to be quite grumpy. He had inflicted bleeding wounds on other members of the family if they dared to attempt to pick him up. He had never drawn blood from me, but he commanded utmost respect. We all loved him and admired his 'spirit' but hastened to warn any unsuspecting visitor, "Don't stroke the cat!" He had the unnerving habit of purring loudly as though he was reveling in your attentions and then without any warning he would turn into some saber-toothed demon. When questioned about his years of tyranny, he blurted out, "Well you cut my balls off, what do you expect!" I then proceeded to apologize for the entire human race and endeavored to explain why we neuter animals – not an easy task!

Chippy was similarly affronted. As I had been guided to do with Zappa, I used my pendulum and visualized removing the trauma around his back end, still locked into his body's cellular memory. He appeared moderately appeased. He then fixed me with a very imperious gaze and explained that he was not trying to bite *Cara*; he was biting the horrible negative energy that was attached to her. Chippy explained that Cara was being bullied at school and was struggling to cope with some of her more unpleasant peers. When I mentioned this, Cara verified that this was the case and she had been feeling very unhappy with the actions of some girls at her school. I worked with Cara, removing the energy and we visualized protective layers to repel any further words or deeds that might be sent consciously or otherwise from the unkind girls. The family took steps with the school to have this serious matter addressed. I told the family that Chippy was doing his best to protect them and felt responsible for their welfare, rather like a philanthropic sovereign. We took care to disguise our amusement of his sense of grandeur. However, I had to admit that he was a very special cat and since working with them to remove the attachment, he has permitted affectionate advances from Cara without any adverse behavior.

I have also worked with cats and some dogs, who suddenly start to mess in the house to alert their owners to negative energies within their environment. Zappa gave me another valuable lesson with this, as twice I entered my front door only to narrowly miss stepping in a foul smelling 'gift' from him. He had always been a meticulously clean cat, so I was very surprised at the first occasion and a little annoyed at the second. Poor Zappa, he must have wondered why he had decided to share his life with me as I was so dim-witted. I was so puzzled that I rang my shaman friend, who immediately educated me as to what my wise cat was doing. Apparently animals can attempt to cleanse negative energy, or certainly alert us to do something about it. I had no idea that a negative energy was there, so I had a lot of groveling to do once again.

When I receive calls from owners who are having this problem and there are no medical reasons for these apparent transgressions, I frequently intuit the negative energies and trapped spirits in the house. Once these are lifted, the caring cat or dog resumes its formerly clean behavior.

Cats are especially affected by anxiety and stress in the family and will often mess if they are trying to alert their owners that their stress levels are becoming too high and they need to address their issues. Unfortunately some of the stress comes from having to clear up mess. However, they are only trying to tell us that the negativity from our stress is becoming difficult to live with. I always ask owners who contact me on this subject, what is going on for them in their lives and if there has been any extra stress occurring of late.

Animals, like people are also affected by ley lines that may run through our property. People have dowsed the directions of these lines and monitored the effects on houses and their occupants. The animals can soon alert us to any disruptive energy 'hot spots'.

Another amazing case of this was when I first met Jenny and Tony.

They had been experiencing some horrific accidents on the farm with their cows and horses and there seemed to be several occurrences of incidents that appeared to be really bad luck. It seemed that if something could go wrong, it would do.

An expert in earth energies had been brought in to dowse and clear the leyline that affected the farm and other inhabitants of the village as it ran through their houses. Ill health and accidents seemed rife. Since the energy lines had been cleared, things did seem a lot calmer and stable on the farm.

About a year later at Jenny's farm, the cows had begun to object going into the parlour to be milked and were displaying similar behaviour as to when the leyline had been so 'polluted' with negative energy. It had become a real battle to get the cows to take up their normal positions in the herringbone structure of the parlour. Cows are normally very docile and know exactly their individual place in the procession of milkers entering the parlour and routinely chose which particular part of the parlour to me milked in. However, even the most normally accommodating cow was now showing signs of stress and fear of entering the parlour. I was asked by Jenny to help clear the people and animals that were possibly carrying residual negative energy from the effects of the ley line. This included herself, as she had experienced very unpleasant sensations when milking her cows in the 'pit' of her parlour.

Not knowing anything of the direction of the leyline, I intuited, with the help of a drum, a line about two feet thick that run almost straight through the middle of the parlour. I noticed the tone of the drum change either side of the line. I cleansed the line with white sage using the traditional Native American technique 'smudging', or purifying with fragrant smoke from smouldering herbs, and visualized placing what I call light crystals deep into the ground. I visualized the large crystals shining their pure light down the leyline, clearing any dark energy. These are pure energy and I will describe their healing properties later.

Jenny confirmed that the area I had found was the same place where the previous dowser had discovered the leyline. I am not sure why the negative energy returned to the leyline. Perhaps there were some negative influences that were affecting the line further down the country. It has been documented that the energies of people can greatly influence these lines through the years. However the clever cows had felt the ill effects of this and had alerted us in time to prevent a return to the awful incidents that had previously plagued the village. Once the line had been cleared, the cows resumed their routine nonchalance of the twice daily milking.

Power Animals

I was lucky enough to be helped by animals that came in an energy form, which the Native Americans call Power Animals. Visualizing and utilizing the strengths of an individual animal is common practice with shamanic work. I am often helped by 'power animals' in my own healing work, and feel that they are re-awakening my past life skills. I am fortunate to have two wonderful lions that help remove particularly unpleasant energies; one male lion and a lioness who I feel protect me from any negative influences. Many different species come to help whenever their particular services are required.

I was once working with a lovely woman who was feeling very depressed because she could not conceive and have a much wanted child. I sensed that she had been 'beating herself up' and her self-esteem was greatly diminished, so she was becoming very disempowered. The negative energy of her berating seemed to have gathered like energy 'barbs' in her solar plexus and sacral energy centres which related to personal power and self-esteem and her validation as a woman.

I was astounded to feel the presence of an enormous female hyena enter the room to assist me. Again, I had to put trust in my guidance and know that I always had the intent for working in the light, for the very highest good of all and always asked for the very purest guidance. To find an awesome ferocious looking creature as my healing colleague was astonishing. Even more astonishing was that the woman could feel the energy barbs being gently removed by the creature, which then proceeded to spit them out through the window where they transmuted into what looked like little lengths of white silk ribbon. This may sound like some chemical induced hallucination, but I knew what I was visualizing and the message from the Hyena was that she had come to give this woman strength. Although Hyenas generally get a bad 'press', they are fiercely protective mothers and succeed in rearing their young, despite very harsh conditions. The Hyena wanted to instil self-esteem and re-empower the woman to believe in herself.

I have had so many wonderful creatures, too numerous to mention, aiding my sessions that I am so grateful and pleasantly surprised as to which creature is willing to help me. Their particular strengths are always totally appropriate to the case in hand. Of course I have to use my discretion as to which clients may be open to the fact that there is more than one healer working with them!

Rocco the German shepherd

Rocco was another very sensitive dog that was susceptible to energies. Walking him through the ancient town where he lived proved to be extremely difficult. He seemed to balk and bark at invisible fears and his owner was truly perplexed and rather tired of her arm being nearly torn from its socket. He also was terrified at bangs and the rumblings of thunder – which is quite common in many dogs, but his behavior was extreme. He told me that in a past life he had been a sniffer dog in the war and that there had been an explosion with the bomb disposal team and many people had been killed. He showed me that in that life he had been black and gold, much darker than his present coloration. He had been used to sniff out the bodies of the victims. So it seemed that in this life he was still finding the energies of people that had died and was very troubled by trapped spirits that were energetically still pervading the town.

There had been a spirit presence in the house that kept moving objects and turning on the television in the middle of the night. Rocco had woken his owners to tell them that the television was on. They were dismayed to find it blaring away in the lounge where they knew they had definitely switched it off earlier. This happened on more than one occasion, much to the annoyance of the owners. Rocco told me that there was a lady who had died there, who was very cross because the house had been altered, rather like Dudley's. When I tuned into her she kept saying, "Where am I going to put the table?"

Rocco was doing his best to alleviate and alert everyone's attention to this trapped spirit. As before, a pillar of light was created and the spirit was invited to leave.

I worked to help Rocco be less sensitive and affected by negative energies and giving him a protective layer rather like Parker's, so that he had some defense against his fearful encounters. He was a beautiful dog and thankfully his owner was very receptive to the explanation of his behavior. He is gradually becoming calmer and glad that at least he doesn't have to share his home with too many spooks!

CHAPTER 6

Psychic Surgery and Light Crystal Healing

The term psychic surgery for me may differ from other people's ideas. There are some amazing psychic surgeons who perform incredible feats of healing, but I feel there are also some people who are not entirely genuine. I do not profess to reach into an animal or person's body and extract physical tissue. The way that I have been guided is to visualize using appropriate 'tools' to alleviate symptoms. This can seem very strange, even for me. It is using the power of the mind to move and change energy. Again, I have the animals to thank for teaching me what they need in order to heal.

The main healing tools I use are what I call 'light crystals'. They are pure energy and do not exist as a physical reality. Whenever I am working with people or animals, I always ask for the method of healing which will respect and empower them for the very highest good of the client. On many occasions, light crystals in many shapes and sizes have been given to me energetically, to place within or around the body or in the environment in space clearing work. I usually visualize the light crystal being placed in the palm of my hand and they can be used in various ways, depending on the specific needs of the client. I feel that I may have used these crystal healing techniques in a previous incarnation and rather like the shamanic methods I use, they have been re-awakened within me.

One of the greatest spiritual 'gifts' of my mother's passing was that in my desperation to help alleviate her pain and my distress at her awful prognosis, I was reminded of ancient healing tools that I had once used. Watching anyone or any creature you love, suffer, is excruciatingly heart breaking as anyone who has cared for a terminally ill patient will tell you. Added to this, the fact that I was supposed to be a healer and could not heal or save my own mother was devastating. However, we all die, our time comes to us all, and I now understand that my role was to help her pass as painlessly and gracefully as possible, without any fear. I feel that one of the greatest gift we can give is to help ease someone's passing when their time to move to another phase of their soul's journey, has come.

I lay in bed one night imploring the universe to help me lessen the pain she was experiencing. She was suffering with a large tumour that was compressing and so restricting the bowel. This was causing terrible pain. I was guided to visualize her bowel rather like a mine shaft that was caving in and I was 'given' what looked like 'pit props' to support the roof and sides of the mine shaft. I was surprised that my pit props did not look wooden; they looked as though they were made of something like quartz crystal, with an inner fire that shone out and illuminated the whole of the symbolic tunnel.

I concentrated hard and prayed that in some fantastic way this might ease her pain. To my amazement when I spoke to my mother the next morning she said that she had felt some relief, so the next night I visualized examining the strength of the symbolic mine shaft again. I was worried to see that although the pillar like 'props' were holding up the tunnel roof, the shaft was in danger of collapsing behind them. So I placed more light crystal pillars along the length of the tunnel and hoped that this would give enough support to prevent collapse. This seemed to have quite a miraculous effect on her and although, sadly, her health deteriorated in other ways, she never experienced that awful pain again.

After she died, her doctor remarked at how surprising it had been that she had not had any more pain from that tumour. I secretly prayed that I had helped somehow. I have studied psycho-neuro-immunology where the mind is used as a healing tool, visualizing symbolic images creating positive change. These techniques have had great success in cancer help centres and it seemed logical to me that if we can make ourselves ill through stress and negative thought, surely we have the ability to 'think' ourselves well. However, creating positive healing images within others was previously not in my brief.

Several months later, one of my human clients suddenly announced that they had been hearing a message for me from one of their guides. I was quite taken aback as this was a very down to earth person, not normally prone to talking about spirit guides, but they seemed completely unfazed. The message was that I had to believe in the power of my healing tools and that the 'light crystals' did work. They went on to say that I had to work to discover more about them and to use the light crystals far more. Obviously the person had no knowledge of the way I had tried to help my mother and I had certainly never mentioned light crystals, as I was still not entirely sure of their efficacy. This was quite emotional for me as I realised some of the deeper reasons for my mother's passing and that perhaps there was some karmic contract to help each other on our soul journeys.

I felt that I had to honor her by utilizing the knowledge she had re-awakened in me. So I hoped that I would be guided to use these etheric crystals whenever appropriate.

Les the Racehorse

I was called to see Les as I had been told he had hurt his back and he was in a bad way and his future in racing was doubtful. As I entered the paddock, I didn't need to have any telepathic powers to interpret the look he gave me. His lithe bay frame was hunched and his belly looked 'tucked up', which is what horses do when they are stressed or in pain. The anguish in his eyes said "Don't even breathe near me..."

A back therapist had been called in, but Les was in such distress that they felt that he was in too much pain to even touch. Apparently Les had tried to turn round whilst in a horse box trailer and had got completely wedged. After a great struggle his owners had somehow managed to extricate him, but his back was terribly painful. I knew he would react quite dangerously if I attempted to touch him and I didn't want to distress him any further. He was having great difficulty walking and displayed a cringing, shuffling gait. Not being the tallest person in the world, I stretched as far as I could, in order to 'feel' his energy about two inches above his back, without touching him.

I had allowed him to smell some relaxing drops I use, that contain essential oils and crystal essences. They create a safe space to work emotionally and in cases like this, they help to physically calm the client. He seemed to calm a little, but he glared at me warily in case I attempted to touch his back. I kept talking to him and reassuring him that I was not going to touch him. I felt heat in an area of imbalance in his back and I was guided to visualize massaging some cooling gel into the affected area. It was as if I had to imagine dipping my fingers into a pot of gel and massaging it into his back. I was surprised to 'see' that here were tiny particles of light crystal in the gel which gave it an appearance of a substance rather like glitter glue! This was the first time I had been shown anything like this so I felt very silly, pretending to dip my fingers in the pot and then proceed to massage thin air above Les's back. Goodness only knows what the owner must have thought! However, when I finished my extraordinary procedure, to my astonishment, his eyes seemed calmer and softer somehow and when we took off his halter and he walked away from us, I thought he looked less pained. Perhaps it was just wishful thinking, or just my imagination, but his whole body language seemed to have changed. I couldn't quite believe that my imaginary 'glitter glue' had worked, but his owner agreed that he was definitely moving better. We discussed the homeopathic remedies he was being given, which I'm sure helped, but his dramatic improvement continued and only days later he was back to his cheeky self. After gentle convalescing he resumed his racing career much to the delight of the owner.

Bonito's Discs

Bonito was a beautiful Hanoverian dressage horse, he had suffered back problems for quite a while and together with emotional issues, and he was not reaching his potential.

When I first visited him he was extremely anxious and he told me he was worried as he thought I might be a prospective buyer and he didn't want to leave his home and his lovely owner. He had changed homes several times in his life and he was loathe to have to adjust to yet another owner and different regime. I reassured him that I was there to help and to understand his concerns. He had had his back treated but had not seemed to enjoy his treatment. I used my pendulum to dowse his back to intuit the area of imbalance. I was guided to place three small light crystal 'discs' in his spine and then visualize rotating them into very specific positions. I felt that he was telling me exactly where he wanted them and how to position them. I had begun to get used to doing as I was told telepathically by a horse.

The feedback from his owner was that he was greatly improved and was beginning to enjoy his work far more with much more propulsion. He also seemed far more content in himself. I had asked his owner to keep telling him telepathically how much she loved him and to reassure him that she would never sell him. She adored him so I knew he could believe her. Their relationship deepened over the next few months. So much so, that after attending one of my animal communication workshops, Bonito's owner was practicing her newly acquired skills and was surprised at a message he had for her. They had been working hard on their dressage techniques and she had been experiencing back pain. Bonito said in no uncertain terms that his owner needed to pay me a visit to have her own light crystal 'discs' put in. She duly made an appointment to see me and I obliged by placing discs in her lower back, exactly the way that Bonito had guided me to previously. His owner said that her back did feel better, so I hoped they would have many pain free future rides together.

Ted's Embarrassment

I fell in love with a wonderful character called Ted. He was a bold bay horse in Jenny's hunt hire yard. He had a problem peeing and his urine was cloudy and had a strong smell. His 'flow' was also impeded and irregular. This was the first of many bizarre cases where animals have trained me in healing. I was guided to imagine an endoscope that could pass up through his sheath and urethra and determine the cause of his little problem. As with Les I never actually touched him, but indicated with my finger about an inch from his sheath. To my amazement I visualized my finger entering his sheath and traveling upwards into his body as it grew longer. Although I knew I was only visualizing doing this, the funniest thing was that he seemed to be feeling the intrusion. He turned his head towards me as though asking what on earth I was playing at. I explained what I was doing to Jenny, who luckily was used to me and was never surprised by my peculiar visions. We agreed that Ted was looking embarrassed as he gave us rather disapproving looks.

I intuited that there were some tiny crystal like formations that were causing problems, so the end of my finger changed from being like an endoscope into becoming a laser and I visualized zapping the crystals. I had no idea if this would help, I just followed my instructions. As I mentally removed my long finger, we again saw a reaction from Ted. We both felt that he had definitely known what was going on, however weird it had been.

We turned Ted out to graze and I telepathically asked him to show us if the procedure had helped, by peeing if he felt better. He took several strides into the field and I thought for a moment he had ignored my request, then suddenly he stopped, turned to look at me and I swear he almost winked. He then proceeded to stretch out his legs, taking up the normal position of a gelding peeing and passed clear urine with no trouble, effortlessly. He groaned in melodramatic relief, nodded at us once, and then nonchalantly strode off up the paddock to search for the best grass. I vowed to always trust what I was being told, however mad it might seem.

Ebony's Burst Blood Vessel

Another time my middle finger 'laser' was called for was with a horse called Ebony, whose main issues I will illustrate in the next chapter. He had been out hunting and had been galloping flat out. Unfortunately he had burst a blood vessel and had bled profusely out of his left nostril. The bleeding had finally abated, but it was causing concern lest this frightening episode should reoccur during demanding exercise in future. Again I was guided to place my middle finger very gently up into the nostril and visualize it extending up into the head and cauterizing a blood vessel. I hoped this would prevent any further problems. This seemed to work as this has never troubled him again. I never quite know how well my remedial intuitive methods will work; I just pray that they help.

More Trouble with Parker

Since Parker had made new friends now that he no longer possessed his 'black cloud' and green slime, he had begun training in earnest. He was much fitter and more confident the next time I saw him and all had been well until he had been really asked to fully extend his paces and gallop further distances. Unfortunately he seemed to run out of 'puff' and was forced to pull up heaving and blowing trying to get more air into his lungs. This was not good news for a race horse where stamina was everything. His shining future was looking doubtful. When he had been examined by the vet it was discovered that the valve in his throat was not functioning properly and the only cure would be a very expensive tie-back operation. This ensures that the valve is fixed in an open, more stable position so that enough air can pass through.

Parker's owners asked if there was anything we could do to help and I had said we would do our best. Once more I enlisted the help of Dave, as this was quite a tricky proposition. Together we visualized using a needle and gold thread and psychically sewed the valve into the correct position. We visualized everything looking pink and healthy with plenty of space for a beautiful air flow. We felt that Parker should only resume his training very slowly over the next few weeks. We braced ourselves when it was deemed the right time to attempt a short gallop. It was not easy to hold him back as Parker was very full of himself and desperate to rev up a few gears. The news was really encouraging, although he made some slightly exaggerated noises in his breathing, he seemed to manage beautifully. We were all so pleased, especially Parker who looked every bit the athlete and wanted to prove his worth. It was decided to attempt a race and he was entered at a course which was it felt would suit him. The day of his first race dawned and all looked well. Parker looked the picture of health and had coped with his gallops well, so was very fit. I was working in another area on the day, so kept praying to myself that his breathing would be fine and he would cope with the ardours of the race.

I was so disappointed to hear that as he had accelerated to take up the lead, he slipped on the bend, badly damaging a tendon and causing him to be pulled up. It was such a shame as his wind was fine and he had no problems with the air flow, which was very gratifying, but we were all devastated at his leg injury, especially as he seemed all set to win the race. Hopefully after several months of rest, he may resume his racing career and needless to say I have got to work on his leg with the light crystals.

Tilley's Support Bandages

Another method of using the light crystals, shown to me by the horses, was in the form of a bandage. I was asked to visualize bandaging the leg, with an elastic bandage that sticks to itself and within the fabric of this were tiny fragments of light crystal that infuse the leg with healing energy.

A lovely mare called Tilley had been harried and chased around her field by another horse that had broken into her normally safe and calm environment. I had worked on her before as she had a symptom called locking stifles, where the hind legs lock above the hocks, causing discomfort and lameness. I intuited that she had a past life injury that was impacting again in the present and after a soul retrieval and healing she recovered well. However, this latest disaster had really aggravated the old problems and both her back legs were locking badly, especially the left hind leg. I was guided to use the light crystal bandages, but as I visualized them being wrapped around the legs they seemed to be needed beneath the surface of the skin, so that they were supporting all the soft tissue internally. It must have looked very strange as I pretended to wrap invisible bandages around Tilley's legs, but they seemed to help her recovery.

Toby the Black Labrador

I was asked to have a chat with a lovely old grey muzzled Labrador called Toby. Since moving into his owner's new house, he seemed to have a distinct aversion to walking on the floor-boards in their hallway and even in the kitchen that had 'wood effect' linoleum. He was petrified of any floor surface that he thought was wooden. This was a problem as getting in and out of the house was a struggle as he was no lightweight. His feed and water bowls were in the kitchen but even the thought of his food did not tempt him to venture across the hall into the kitchen. Their other dog showed no such qualms and was only too eager to assist Toby by scoffing his meal. His desperate owners were dumbfounded as to why he was scared.

Toby showed me a terrible past life trauma where he had been trapped in a house fire and the smoke had been coming up from a lower basement floor through the floorboards. He had desperately tried to get his owners out of the house to safety, by alerting them in their sleep. They had narrowly escaped death, but poor Toby's feet had been scorched. His current owners described how Toby sometimes stood on the front step barking into the hallway as if trying to warn them of some danger. The poor dog's trauma had been triggered by moving to a house with exposed floorboards. He was devoted to his owners and I suspected that they may well have been in that burning house in another life with him, and of course Toby wanted to make sure that everyone was safe.

I removed negative energy from Toby's paws and visualized placing a small light crystal between the pads of each foot. This time the crystals felt soft and malleable, rather like clear plasticine but still with its inner crystal fire. I also used a healing etheric substance for 'packing' wounds of past life injuries that are causing present day physical pain.

I performed a 'soul retrieval' bringing back the traumatized dog from the past in one piece, then set to work placing large light crystals in the floor in the hall and the kitchen.

I also placed a curtain of light crystals in the hall entrance, rather like the beaded curtains used in doorways in hot weather. This was to act as a cleanser of negative energy of anyone entering the house and shine positive healing light all down the hallway. Toby's owners also gave him some flower remedies and gradually he gained courage and enough confidence to venture gingerly across the floorboards. The last feedback I had was that Toby was slowly but surely improving, his fear had been locked inside him for so long that it took a little time to release and realize that he need never endure such a horrific event ever again.

Sun Discs

Another tool that I have been given to work with to help with the negative effects of energy drain from one person to another, or the dynamic between an owner and their animal, are what I call Sun Discs. They originate from my Egyptian heritage and were the symbol of the 'Aten'. The Sun Discs are gold and beautifully symmetrical and can vary in size, rather like the light crystals, depending on the job in hand.

I was first shown their healing properties when I was in Sedona and I was with a friend anchoring energy in specific sites around the area, also in the Grand Canyon.

I was guided to visualize placing these large discs in an arc to reflect light and to transmute negative energy throughout one of the main valleys in Sedona, where there are supposed to be many vortexes of energy.

These first discs, used for earth healing, were huge, just pure energy. They help to transmute negative energy into a purer form. When working to create a safe barrier between two people or an animal and their owner, they are about two feet in diameter. When Dave the shaman intuits a problem between two people, where one is being drained by the other, he rings me and asks me to 'put a sun disc in'.

I recently used a cleansing soft sun disc to act as a sort of circular cat flap for a cat that was experiencing a lot of negativity in the home and was messing in the house, causing even more stress to the household. I had to visualize placing a sun disc between the owner and the cat and this other special 'cat flap' at the back door, so the cat could walk through and be cleansed of the negativity in the house and be strengthened as it re-entered. Strange as it might sound, it seemed to work, as the cat immediately stopped messing in the house, the owner seemed far less stressed and worried about the cat, and I was thrilled because my new adaptation of my sun discs, seemed to be really effective. The cat's owner and I had been emailing each other for a couple of weeks, with updates on the progress of the cat's behaviour and before putting the sun discs in place, it had been a case of one step forwards and two steps back. Just when I thought my space clearing at the house had worked, or my efforts to reassure the cat telepathically, had worked, he would go and pee and pooh again. But I am glad to say that from then on, I had one triumphant email and all seems to be peace and harmony now.

Healing the Environment

I was asked by my veterinary friend Judith to visit a stud farm where she had been treating the mares and pregnancy testing. She was concerned because so many animals had died and a gorgeous thoroughbred mare had aborted her foal after eight months gestation, which was heartbreaking. Judith was concerned because there were huge electricity pylons carrying very high voltage cables through the farm. Although it has been stated that proximity to pylons may be a factor in blood disorders and occur-rences of cancer, I'm not sure whether it has been scientifically proven that this is directly correlated to health problems, but there were an inordinate number of casualties on the farm. I visited the farm and met all the beautiful horses and their foals. The horses all felt very much loved and their owners cared for them deeply. The people seemed to be fairly healthy and the mare that aborted previously had finally managed to conceive again and so far seemed very happy in her pregnancy. I was alarmed to find that the pylons ran right through the paddocks where the horses grazed and the crackling of the cables was most disturbing. I consulted my friend Dave, who suggested visualizing copper hoops encircling the wires, to cut off the electromagnetic waves escaping and affecting the area. The next morning I awakened at 5am and was guided to do what was needed at the farm. It took ages visualizing remotely wrapping the cables but eventually I felt I had completed that task. I then visualized a structure like a circus safety net encrusted with tiny light crystals that ran along underneath the encircled cables, connected at each pylon. I was then guided to place large light crystals in two lines in the ground, like a flight path adjacent to the overhead lines of the cables. I wished I could have received this guidance a little later in the morning than 5am! However, I truly hoped that it would help to counter the negative effects of the cables and that no further deaths would occur.

It has amazed me how the light crystal energy has evolved in my awareness over time. Each case teaches me so much and I am so grateful to all my tutors. In severe cases I have been shown in a meditation that I can create a healing amphitheatre that I can turn into an entire light crystal structure. In healing visualizations I place very serious cases within the structure and visualize the floor and walls giving off healing light, so that any person or animal lying on the floor gets the light permeating all through and around them. I feel this is another part of my past life history showing me past healing skills that have resurfaced into my consciousness, thanks to the discovery of my mother's 'pit props'.

I hope that my healing intent will benefit all that I place within the etheric structure.

Healing with Dolphins

I have also been guided to place light crystals of different kinds in different parts of the world, aided and abetted by my cetacean friends that I've travelled the world to work with. Whilst visiting the Azores, I stayed on Pico Island where we were lucky enough to swim with many species of dolphin: Bottlenose, Spotted, Riso and Common. We also encountered huge sperm whales and pilot whales traveling in pods. The Azores are a fantastic place for experiencing incredibly diverse species as it seems to be a well worn route for them to pass through the planet's oceans.

Before I set off on my journey from England to the Azores, I had a dream. In this dream I saw a bottlenose dolphin come right up to me and take a light crystal from my hand and then dive down to the bottom of the sea and place the crystal into the oceanic grid. I believe there are grid systems all around the earth that need repairing or strengthening for planetary healing. So I awoke from my wonderful dream that had seemed so real, full of optimism that this might indeed occur in reality. Every day that went by during my stay where I failed to meet my dolphin, I became more and more disappointed and a sense of failure overcame me. It had seemed such an important premonition, I felt sure the dolphins wanted me to fulfill my part of the healing to help the planet. Right at the end of my stay when I was becoming really despondent and despairing of ever finding the special creature, I was given a good 'talking to'. My guides told me to stop pushing so hard and to trust that I had made the connection with the dolphin, so healing was already taking place. I tried to be more positive after this and actually enjoy the rest of my stay. On the last morning that I was with the group of people swimming with dolphins, just as we were about to leave the deep blue ocean, we were treated to an incredible sight.

A super pod of Bottlenose dolphins gave us the most wonderful send off as 300 dolphins swam past our small boat. The sea seemed to turn into a vast cauldron of bubbling water as the dolphins leapt and frolicked past our astonished faces. It was almost as if they were saying goodbye to us and had come out in force. It is a sight I will never forget. I felt that nothing could ever top that experience, but I was wrong. I had booked to stay an extra day as it was my birthday and I couldn't think of a better way of celebrating than going on a whale watching trip to pay my final respects to the wonderful creatures. We were given the gift of seeing a calf and mother Sperm whale breaching and crashing back down into the foam and spray of the ocean. We saw a feeding frenzy of dolphins, leaping and attacking a large fish ball. Shearwater birds screamed and dived down to gobble up any fish that had survived the dolphin attack. This spectacle has been filmed in wildlife programs at the same location in the presence of Mount Pico steadily gazing down.

I had been guided to visit the mountain earlier in the day to place crystals there which had been an awesome experience and I little realised that it was just a prelude to what was to come later in the day. We were again just about to say goodbye to the ocean for the last time when we came across a small pod of Pilot whales. Their black bullet-shaped bodies effortlessly cruising through the water, made us sit up in excitement. They were so close. We had tried to keep our distance from the whales so as not to be intrusive, but these whales seemed happy to swim near us. One whale in particular seemed to glue himself to the side of the boat where I was lucky enough to be sitting.

Eventually it dawned on me that he was making contact. I had been sending all the love I could out to the whales, as I had with all the wonderful creatures we had encountered. This whale seemed to be looking at me, until I finally got the message, "Give me the crystal". So I asked to be 'given' a light crystal that the whale could take to the oceanic floor. I visualized the most beautiful orb that was taken by the whale. I watched him diving down and down, deeper and deeper through the clear water. I somehow knew that this whale was fulfilling my healing intent and huge feelings of emotion welled up in me and I hoped that in some small way, the crystal would help their endangered environment and fragile ecosystems. What a wonderful birthday present and what a privilege to be helped by such a fantastic creature. I was later to experience many more wonderful encounters where the cetaceans helped me, which I will tell you about in a later chapter.

CHAPTER 7

Blueprints, Hoof Prints, Paw Prints and Foot Prints!

I was taught another healing exchange and once again the animals were my tutors in the strange technique that involved what I visualized as a blue line that contoured the body. It was quite a fine line and I was told that it represented the blue print of the animal's soul journey. This could contain dents and fractures which represented past injuries.

Ru/Rupert

The first occasion this happened was when I was called by Joan to see her beautiful chestnut gelding Ru. She had asked me to visit, because he was displaying quite challenging behaviour and was not an easy ride. He seemed permanently stressed and anxious. He had been sold many times to different homes as none of his previous owners had managed to cope with him. Joan felt that Ru was testing her to see if she was also going to fail. Hearing about his antics, I agreed that she was indeed being sorely tested.

Joan had decided that she was determined to get to the bottom of Ru's behaviour and she had vowed that she would never sell him. She hated the fact that he had had so many homes and he was such a beautiful horse with so much unfulfilled potential. She didn't want to give up on him, but she was running out of options. Some owners might have considered destroying him as he was so unsafe, but I knew that Joan was trying to explore every avenue to avoid that terrible fate.

When I entered his loose box, he had a wild expression and was very agitated. I tried to send reassuring, calming thoughts to him, hoping that he would allow me to work with him. He kept saying to me in my head, "It's my legs, it's my legs."

Eventually as I placed my hands on him he began to calm and as I intuited his energy around his body. I was amazed to find that

Ru

when I looked intuitively at his front legs they seemed to be missing from below his knees. It was almost as if where his legs and hooves should be, there were dotted lines, with the symbolic energy of phantom limbs.

I mentioned this to Joan as tactfully as I could and she said it was strange, as another therapist had worked on Ru and had commented that he didn't seem grounded at all in his front legs.

Ru showed me a horrific past life death where he had been ridden into battle by a warrior who was trying to defeat what looked like Samurai fighters. The Samurai opponent had chopped off Ru's front legs in order to bring his rider down where he could be decapitated. This was disturbing to witness and poor Ru had carried this trauma so long.

When I asked for guidance, I was amazed to be given what looked like a small blue crayon. I had to visualize joining up the dots around where his legs should have been and re-draw them! I duly did as I was told and imagined holding the pen and physically pretended to draw his legs. This was another occasion when I felt in danger of finding a firm hand on my shoulder and being led away by some men in white coats!

However, Ru's eyes calmed considerably when I performed his soul retrieval. He had shown me that he was a magnificent black horse with a flowing mane and tail with a somewhat bigger build than his present physical form. This beautiful horse energetically flowed through me, back into Ru and I prayed again that I might have helped.

All seemed to be going well between Joan and Ru until a couple of months later, I had an SOS from her. Apparently Ru had kicked her. Nothing was broken but she was severely bruised and battered around her side and had narrowly missed having her hip broken.

I had hoped they would progress well and enjoy many happy years together. This most recent faux pas by Ru was really putting a strain and casting some doubt on their future.

When I arrived at the yard, I was greeted by deafening shouts in my head from Ru. All he kept shouting was "Rupert, Rupert!" I had no idea what he meant, but the moment I mentioned this to Joan, she promptly burst into tears.

Rupert had been a horse that Joan had owned who had died in her arms. She was still holding incredible grief from his loss as she felt he should have been saved and his death could have been prevented by proper treatment of his condition. Ru told me that he was Rupert and he had found his way back to Joan in order to heal their karma. We were both feeling very emotional by now as we were awed at the journey that Ru had taken and how they had obviously been destined to be reunited. I felt that Ru had really wanted to be sure that Joan was ready to let go of her grief and be healed, but it was a rather dramatic and painful way of alerting us.

Joan tried to accept this and we discussed how this could be true. I was amazed to find that in Ru's equine passport his name was spelt Ru. I had always previously assumed that it was Roo, but we thought that Ru could be an abbreviation for Rupert. Joan had had no input at naming him as he had been named at birth, several years before. She had never made any connection between Ru and his predecessor until then and we agreed it was a pretty close coincidence. I am glad to say that Ru is a reformed character and Joan is enjoying her second chance at happier times with her beautiful horse.

Ebony

Before I worked on poor Ebony's burst blood vessel with my Zappy finger, I had a much more serious task to perform and I still feel that it was the biggest re-building job I have ever done.

Ebony had taken to suddenly bolting in sheer terror and had caused serious injury to a cyclist that he had knocked off his bike. Ebony had ditched his rider and charged blindly through the village with no care for his safety or others. He was such a sweet horse and I knew there must be some deep seated reason for his dangerous behaviour. Like Woody, I felt this horse was not naturally unsafe or wanted to hurt anyone, but nevertheless he was in danger of being destroyed.

Ebony

His large sad eyes seemed to look deep into my soul as though pleading with me to understand his terror. He was a beautiful horse and his dark fur shone as though it had been polished like the wood of his namesake.

I gently asked him to show me a time when his terror began. The first thing I felt was the terrible sound of terrified trumpeting. Then I 'saw' in my head what Ebony was describing. The trumpeting was coming from a rampaging elephant that was fleeing from a tiger that had suddenly turned on its hunters who were positioned in a wicker basket framework on its back. This was many years ago in India.

Ebony showed me that he was then a fine, light boned bright bay horse with the most beautiful curvy ears typical of the horses indigenous to India. Unfortunately his ears were the problem as the sound of the elephant struck him with terror and he bolted.

His unfortunate rider fell off but was saved from a far worse fate as Ebony charged, too late to realize his mistake, straight over a cliff. His body was smashed on the rocks below and I was shown his shattered 'blueprint'. As I looked at him standing in front of me in his stable he still seemed to be fractured, almost like a 'crackle glaze' effect.

I had to imagine somehow joining all the smashed pieces together like a precious vase and literally re-build his outline. I had to concentrate for a long time, which was very demanding. My poor brain was on overtime. However, armed with my blue pen and psychic glue, I managed to get everything reconnected and whole again. This was another case of me wondering if anything had been put in my tea! But all I knew was that it seemed to have a wonderful effect on Ebony.

I blew back the healed bay horse into him and then he turned to give me almost the most emotional moment of my life. He placed his muzzle next to my face and opened his lips and softly held the lower part of my face with them. For a tiny second I wondered if it was wise to let him do this, as potentially he had the strength to inflict serious damage. However, that feeling instantly disappeared as I began to feel his loving intent. He began to blow his soft breath into my nostrils and we spent several minutes, exchanging breath. The intensity of his love and gratitude that poured into me was overwhelming. Tears poured down my face as I was overcome with the sheer power of the love that was being exchanged. This was the sublime moment that gave me the title of this book and defined the ethos of my work. Some time later a friend and colleague remarked on a similar exchange that occurred. She described it as the Divine Thank you, which is exactly what it felt like, touching something so deep within us, binding our souls. As we exchanged breath we became as one, inhaling and exhaling our life giving force.

Ebony was never a novice ride but channeled his speed and vivacity into more constructive activities like cross country jumping. It seemed as though high-pitched sound was the trigger that had brought back all his fears from his past life trauma. The sound of a hunting horn or a cat scarer that we discovered later was emitting high frequency sound from a neighbouring property, was the cause of his fright. After working on releasing his fear of these kinds of sound, he was a much happier and safer horse.

Painting and Decorating - Tramp's Blueprint

About a year later I was asked to visit Tramp. He was on loan to Chester's lovely owner Jane, as a pony for her children to ride. He was a very self possessed little chap. His woolly white fur ruffled in the breeze and his soft pale muzzle sniffed my hand. Jane and I had been working on some of her past life traumas with Chester, but it appeared that there was also some 'history' between Tramp and Jane as well. It was no coincidence that they had found each other again in order to heal some unresolved issues between them. Since attending my animal intuitive and communication workshops, Jane was becoming incredibly sensitive to the needs of the animals companions in her care. She had experienced a horrific flash back to a past life where Tramp was a large white mule and for some reason he had been tethered or caught up on a railway line, unable to escape. Something had happened to Jane to prevent her from retrieving and rescuing Tramp from his plight and he had been hit and killed by the train. Tramp did not expand on this to me as I felt that it was something that had to be worked through between them.

I was guided though to repair his shattered blueprint, which he showed me quite clearly, but this time I was given a large paintbrush as my healing tool. It looked as if it had been dipped in light blue paint and I was 'told' to visualize sloshing the blue paint with the large brush all over his body! This was certainly much quicker than trying to piece each fragment back together. So with mild amusement I carried out my instructions. I had given up questioning my guidance long ago, as I had learnt to trust that however crazy it seemed, it was always appropriate and I endeavoured to carry out my tasks to the best of my ability. As I had finished my psychic painting, the image of the mule seemed much more substantial and I was able to return it into Tramp.

Jane was carrying much guilt and grief from that time so we worked to clear the limiting emotions with Emotional Freedom Technique. This works incredibly well remotely, as proxy EFT on animals and people. This is where a therapist is able to release trapped emotions for the client. I was so proud of Jane, having the courage to address these issues as she had certainly experienced a traumatic past with her animals, but here they were in the present helping to heal all the past pain between them.

Jane, Chester and Tramp seem to be progressing really well. The small pony is a hard task master and always alerts Jane to anything that she is not understanding about their collective needs. As usual the animals are our teachers and we have so much to learn about the capacity to love despite previous ill treatment and their compassion for our shortcomings. Dogs are experts at this; many times you will see a rescue dog that has endured so much abuse, still wag its tail and lick its rescuer, still wanting to give affection and to please.

Jane recently acquired a rescued American Bulldog bitch, who has just these gifts and has become an essential member of the family. She oozes love from every pore of her being and practically stole the show at a workshop run at Jane's home, where she gave us so much love and fun. Ironically her name is Blossom and I felt that she allowed all of us to Blossom during that special day.

Jess the Collie
Jess the collie was brought to me as I ran a clinic on a farm near her home. She was having trouble jumping in and out of the Land rover that her owner drove and I noticed that she had a slightly restricted gait. She was receiving conventional veterinary care,

but she was slow to improve. I suggested that a homeopathic vet may be able to help. However, I did notice that her spine, just before her pelvic area seemed out of balance and as I tuned in deeper, I could see a broken fragment of her blueprint about six inches long. I imagined re-drawing the blue line and placed some 'light crystals' in her back which I hoped would help.

She showed me a past life when a tree had fallen on her. It seemed strange that this complaint should only surface now, as it was a recent condition in this life. My guidance explained that it had always been a weakness in her and as she worked very hard as a sheep dog, eventually the strain took its toll. I was pleased to hear good news from her owner. He said that Jess was doing really well and was now able to jump up and down with ease. I did wish that perhaps she could take life a little easier, but she was a working dog and there was much work to be done in her home and she loved to use her skills.

Pebbles the Ancient Healer

Before working with Pebbles, I had never encountered a case that showed me past lives where horses had been anything but similar equine species, like zebra, mules, donkeys or Shannon's tiny Eohippus. I am quite open to the belief systems that feel that humans can reincarnate in any form, from a tiny ant to an elephant, but I was not convinced that this could happen and had never had a case that proved this to be so. This all changed when I met Pebbles. My pre-conceived ideas were about to be blown 'out of the water'.

My veterinary friend Judith taught final year students at the Duchy College in Cornwall. She introduced the students to all kinds of complementary therapists who worked holistically with horses. She hoped to expand their awareness and demonstrate that there were all kinds of ways to support and complement conventional medicine. Being wonderfully open minded, she had asked me to give demonstrations of my techniques annually and this was my third demonstration. The first visit had been very emotional for one of the students, who cared for a large grey horse called Reuben that we worked on, when his past life trauma surfaced. This illustrated beautifully how deep traumas of our past connections resonate within us.

Judith had described my work, healing past life traumas in animals and people, and I was the last in a varied list of complementary practioners that had visited this particular crop of students. They had been given handouts to prepare them for my slightly alternative approach but none of us were prepared for what Pebbles had to divulge.

She was a fairly aged bay cob that belonged to Judith and we all crowded into her stable, having first begged permission to work with her. She nonchalantly agreed and seemed to scan us all, as one by one, we filed into her domain. I started my usual dialogue, explaining my techniques and how we all have telepathic communication skills innate within us and how past life traumas can impact on present day challenges, either emotionally or physically.

All seemed to be going well until... Pebbles turned to look at me as I was channeling energy up through her body, intuitively scanning her energy centres. I had my hand on the dock of her tail and was concentrating on intuiting any blockages, when suddenly I heard her voice in my head. "I was a master of Eastern medicine and I've come back as a horse to teach Judith new ways of healing and to expand her awareness."

I was so shocked and not a little concerned as to how I was to relay this information to my expectant students, who were waiting for me to give my findings on Pebbles' body scan. I had the feeling that perhaps one or two of them already thought I was a little deranged, goodness only knew what this latest revelation would do to my credibility.

As if this were not enough bizarre information for them to absorb, Judith who had been standing on the other side of Pebbles with me, with her hand resting lightly on the mare's shoulder, suddenly announced, "Oh my god I've just left the planet – Pebbles is taking me on a journey through space!"

This was a first for Judith as she had been a little reticent in accepting details of my outer planetary experiences. Obviously the time had come for us both to be educated. I fully expected the students to all file out of the stable quicker than they had filed in, but to their credit they all stayed to listen to the rest of the demonstration as I somehow continued.

It was quite daunting to be communicating with such a wise sentient being that showed me what the man in her previous incarnation had looked like. Pebbles also showed me detailed diagrams of strange charts of the human body, with what looked like meridian lines, pertinent to Eastern healing methods.

I believe that most animals are far more than they outwardly appear to be, but Pebbles was exceptional. I felt that I was light years away from comprehending the depth of her knowledge and felt very humbled. I continued the best way that I could, working on some physical conditions that I had picked up in her present form as a horse.

Judith finally returned to earth from her galactic reverie, with an expression of deep peace. She had recently developed a deep thirst for knowledge and was expanding her work with homeopathy. I felt that she had a more than able healing colleague to call upon at any time to help her in her future work.

I tried to convey how honoured we had been to witness this and how in awe I was of this horse's ancient wisdom. I had to admit that the vertical learning curve that had been my life for the last few years, had just shot off the page.

We were all calmed down by the entry of a lovely old black Labrador called Basil who seemed to connect with every student. I felt he was telling them that everything was ok and that they could take whatever they wanted from the experience and maybe just be open to the possibility that a horse could have once been a man.

Bolder and the Cavalry Officer

Bolder was referred to me from an equine Cranial Sacral Therapist, who had worked on some of my cases. This therapist was very in tune with past life issues and although she had worked hard on Bolder and his owner, she still felt there were still some emotional issues that were not being addressed. She felt that more investigation was necessary, but Bolder had not been very forthcoming and had buried his trauma very deep.

He was a huge mountain of a horse, a sleek lithe athlete. He was a very proficient Three Day Event horse with enormous presence. He towered above me in the stable and I felt rather small and insignificant. He seemed very 'switched off' and rather melancholic.

Diane, his owner, explained that he had enormous ability and had been very successful at top class level eventing, but seemed to suddenly disconnect from life altogether, rather like a battery powered toy that had gone flat and needed recharging. Unbeknown to me, when Diane had discussed our forthcoming session with the therapist she had said, "Don't be surprised if Madeleine says Bolder was a man before in another life."

I had never discussed my experience with Pebbles with her, so it was a very strange thing for her to say. Luckily Bolder's owner was very open-minded and only related this to me after the horse had shown me his previous incarnations.

There was obviously a very deep connection between Bolder and Diane, who adored him and felt that he was her soul mate. I saw them together in a past life. Bolder was a white cavalry horse and she was a cavalry officer. Diane had been suffering from back pain but had not felt any pain for a while until she suddenly started to experience shooting pains in her side and back. I intuited that they had been shot and I visualized removing the bullets from Diane, and the pain ceased, to her amazement. Bolder was not so easily appeased.

For the first time in Diane's experience he attempted to bite me. He had never shown any hint of aggression since she had known him, but the anger he displayed towards me was frightening. He promptly apologized telepathically but said that his anger had become intolerable, so he had buried it deep and here I was with my psychic can-opener ready to reveal all his well hidden 'worms'. I tried to reassure Bolder that I was there to help and wanted to facilitate the release of his trauma so that he could finally be happy.

What occurred next was quite shocking. Bolder showed me himself as a man in uniform who had fought a terrible battle. His leg was badly injured, but this was not the worst of it. He told me that his horse had been killed and his two brothers had also perished in the terrible war. By this time Diane, who was holding his halter rope was shaking, trembling with emotion, but I was committed to helping him release all his pain so he could be free of it. I persevered in trying to support him in his anguish. He told me that he had felt such enormous grief and guilt, that he alone had survived, and that he determined to punish himself by reincarnating as a horse so as to endure personally the hardships that we placed our loyal equine servants under. He showed me yet another life as a horse where he had been killed in battle, in yet another attempt to punish himself. Now, at last, it seemed he could finally be at peace with himself by reconnecting with Diane and with help, heal the past. I performed several soul retrievals and eventually his eyes took on a brighter lustre. His demeanour brightened and I felt hopeful that we had facilitated positive change and he could look forward to a more joyous life. As this was such a deep rooted issue, a follow up session was necessary, but I am thrilled by his progress. I also worked with Diane to help her release trauma, so they could both enjoy life to the full.

On my second visit to Diane and Bolder they were very different beings. Diane had decided to give Bolder a much earned rest and he seemed very confused. He had had his shoes removed and he couldn't understand what was going on as he had been so much better and felt really fit and ready to compete. He showed me a small light blue van which I found out belonged to the Farrier. It was as though he couldn't understand why he was going unshod and wanted to get on with his work.

Diane told me that he had never had a holiday and she felt that he needed time to process all his emotional changes and assimilate his new way of guilt free being, without the need to prove anything to himself or others.

This time Bolder showed me more of himself as a man with his terrible limp. But this time he showed me the man symbolically writing a letter describing all his grief as though exorcising himself of his entire trauma.

Bolder began to yawn and yawn, which is a sure sign of emotional release, and I gradually could feel the man's spirit's lifting as he began to smile. Bolder then asked me to return the smiling man into him as a soul retrieval of the healed man. I visualised the holographic man passing through me and into Bolder's shoulder when he stood really close to me.

To my delight I received the most wonderful thank you of a velvety kiss to my face, something that Bolder would never have been open enough emotionally to do previously. After this session he looked so relaxed and ready for his holiday, Diane and I were really pleased and hoped he would enjoy the rest.

CHAPTER 8

Healing with the Chakra Systems

Chakras are wheels of pure energy, which exist in centres mainly up through the spinal column. When working on the physical plane with animals, I visualize sending energy up through the body, intuiting blockages where the energy fails to travel through.

With a horse I will normally stand to the side at the rear and place my hand on the dock of the tail just where it joins the body and send the energy, which feels like a flow of golden liquid, up through the pelvis. If there are any imbalances in the spine and sacral areas the energy will stop and appear blocked. I can then use my pendulum to ascertain the exact area of the back that needs healing. The pendulum begins to swing, indicating some negative energy or imbalance. I then encourage the pendulum to

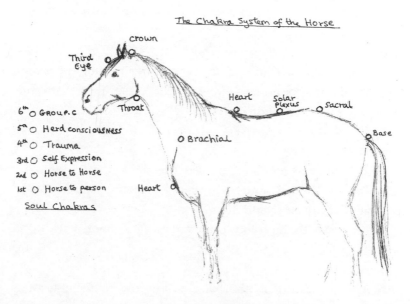

The Chakra System of the Horse

Crown
Third Eye
6th Group.c
5th Herd consciousness
4th Trauma
3rd Self Expression
2nd Horse to Horse
1st Horse to person
Soul Chakras

Throat
Heart
Solar Plexus
Sacral
Base
Brachial
Heart

swing faster and visualize the crystal drawing out the negative energy. I then dip the crystal pendulum in water to cleanse the energy and then return to the specific area to test if the pendulum still shows a negative reaction. When the energy has passed through the pelvic area I then send it through the whole body which allows the golden flow to become like hoops that spiral through the body, checking all the internal organs for emotional or physical imbalance. When the area indicated by imbalance impacts on the corresponding chakra, it can help intuit some of the emotional issues the animal may be carrying. So in this way I am getting information from the body of the animal as well as the animal chatting in my head. Sometimes, like us, they feel off colour but are not always able to indicate why or where. By physically 'feeling' the body it can elaborate on the information I am intuiting from messages from the animal telepathically.

The Chakra Systems of the Horse
There are seven main physical chakras in a horse, as in humans, although they have also shown me higher soul chakras above the head that connect to their higher selves in a more spiritual nature.

Base
Located at the base of the spine. Sense: Smell. Emotion: acceptance, stability, grounding and survival. Associated with the colour red. The element of Earth.

Sacral
Located within the pelvis. Connected to the kidneys, adrenals, reproductive system and lymphatic system. Sense: Taste. Emotion: Identity and validation.
Associated with the colour orange. The element of Water.

Solar Plexus
Located in the centre of the back. Connected to the digestive

system, liver and stomach Sense: Sight. Emotion: self worth issues. Associated with the colour yellow. The element of Fire.

Heart

Located over the chest area and in-between the shoulder blades. Connected with the thymus gland, heart and lungs. Sense: Feel/touch. Emotion: self-love. Associated with the colour pink and the element of element of Air.

Throat

Located in the throat area. Connected to the thyroid gland, throat, ears, nose and mouth. Sense: hearing. Emotion: self- expression. Colour: blue. The element of the Heavens.

Brow/Third Eye

Located in the centre of the forehead. Associated and connected with the pineal gland, sleep and wake states and the brain. Sense: inner knowledge. Emotion: self awareness/intuition. Colour: indigo. The element Silver.

Crown

Located on top of the head. Associated with the pituitary gland, cranial- sacral system, central nervous system, central nervous system, hair and the skin. Sense: thought and connection to the divine. Emotion: spiritual/personal power. Colour Violet. The element Gold.

Brachial

A new chakra has been intuited in the shoulder area which is a common place for physical imbalances in the horse. Located on the side of the body between the neck and the shoulders. Associated with forelegs, chest, head and neck. Sense: instincts.

Colour: black. The element of the Universe. Emotion: empowerment.

I feel that my whole purpose for working with people and animals is to re-empower them to reconnect with their soul journey. So this chakra is very interesting as so many animals take on responsibilities and stresses from their owners. The emotional issues connected with physical problems with shoulders, are all connected to 'shouldering' too much responsibility, so this may be a factor when intuiting problems.

Higher Soul Chakras in Horses

The horses show me these energy centres spinning above the head in a vertical column, rather like spinning balls of white energy. If they are out of balance or in some cases not even formed, it is clear that the spiritual and emotional issues are affecting the wellbeing and harmony of the horse. The way that I have been shown to intuit each chakra is:

Horse to Person

The first ball of energy just above the poll or crown of the head relates to the strength of connection between the horse and humans. If it is out of balance, either sluggish or very faint, then I use the pendulum to activate or clear any imbalance. When working with this chakra, the horse may well tell me of conflicts or abuse from people in the past. These first two soul chakras can interchange depending on the depth of, or lack of, connection with humans eg. a foal that has been reared by humans or a horse that has had poor human contact.

Horse to Horse

The second soul chakra above the first relates to how the horse feels about other horses and how they interact. Imbalances here might indicate self-esteem issues.

Self Expression

The third energy centre above the head relates to how the horse can express itself on a soul level. Is this horse able to fulfill its life purpose?

Trauma Centre

The fourth soul chakra can be full of a conglomeration of past and present life traumas, in which case it can appear very clogged or even black. In this case, I use the pendulum standing next to the horse, visualizing the centre and spin it to draw out and release the offending traumas. This is when a horse may be able to divulge more of its painful past telepathically as I release the dark energy stored in the centre.

Herd Consciousness

The fifth soul chakra is related to the horse's connection to all horses. If this is faint, sluggish or underdeveloped, it indicates that the horse may have confidence issues and will not be good at coping on its own. It may have subconscious feelings of isolation and feel disconnected to its support system.

Group Consciousness

This is connected to what is called the collective consciousness. I believe that this is the awareness of everything that is taking place in the universe or has ever taken place.

Chakra Systems for Dogs and Cats

Dog Soul Chakras:

The five higher soul chakras of the dog are activated and cleared and spun in the same way that I work with the horses.

The first Soul Chakra in dogs relates to **Dog to Person.**

When working with this chakra you can intuit how deep the connections are between the dog and the humans in its life.

The second higher chakra is the **Self Expression** centre.

This is connected to the dog's ability to express itself as a dog – is it empowered enough to be able to express itself appropriately?

The third is the **Trauma** centre.

When feeling into this centre and examining how clear and balanced it is, you can intuit the level of trauma the dog has experienced and past life issues may become apparent, if they have not surfaced from the physical chakras.

The fourth higher centre is the **Pack Consciousness.**

This relates to the connection between the dog and the collective consciousness of the whole canine family. If this chakra is weak, like the horses, it will feel separate, alienated and unsupported. It may be aggressive, as it feels disconnected to any support from its soul companions.

The fifth higher chakra that I have intuited in the dog is the **Collective Consciousness.**

This is how the dog fits in to the big universal picture. Sometimes this centre does not exist in an individual animal, so I visualize creating them as spinning clear wheels of light. Sometimes they exist but are very sluggish or clogged and so take a little time to be sufficiently activated.

Cat Soul Chakras:

Dogs have told me that they have five soul chakras and cats have said they have four. This does not mean that cats are any less connected to the soul purpose, on the contrary they have an almost direct connection with the universe – they have told me jokingly 'nought to the galaxies in six seconds!' Hence the mystical powers traditionally attributed to cats. Again these chakras may need to be created, cleared and spun in harmony with the rest of the energy centres.

Cat to Human Connection
The first chakra is normally connected to the cat's relationship with humans that are most impacting on its life.

Self Expression and Trauma Centre
In cats, the second soul chakra is a combination of self expression and trauma, because aspects of one, deeply affect the other.

The third higher centre involves **Healing and Magic.**

Cats, big and domestic, have a great capacity to transmute negative energy and to give healing. They also connect to metaphysical aspects. They commune with nature spirits and devas and all kinds of beings that are usually beyond our comprehension.

There is a little black cat called Tonic (her sister called Gin was tragically killed). She always appears when I am working at Jenny and Tony's yard and she always indicates which horses need help. I think her name is so appropriate as she really does act as a

Tonic

tonic. She struts along the stable doors making sure I am performing my duties properly.

Galactic / Universal Connection
The final chakra in cats seems to connect to the universe and connections to any planet with healing energies or beings that can help. Little did I realize before, when I had a cuddly moggy sitting on my lap, just what they were capable of and their connections with senior galactic management!

Dowsing
As I've previously mentioned, I use pendulums to work physi-

cally on animals, people and environments, but I also dowse remotely when working with photographs and hair samples. People usually associate the term dowsing with water divining, using long rods that show hidden underground water, which may be in springs, pipes or wells. However many people use pendulums to intuit responses to questions about a person or animal's needs. I use a lapis Lazuli crystal pendulum. The type is called an Egyptian pendulum as it is cut and shaped in a specific way. This is quite a large and heavy pendulum, being crystal, but I find it the best tool for removing negative energies as it is very powerful. Sometimes I can hold the pendulum over a photograph and get extra information about an animal remotely. It also helps with owners questions about feeding and supplements regimes as to their benefits and if the animal likes them! As I described when working in the physical, I can imagine placing my hand at the dock area of the body and sending the energy up through remotely. I can then intuit blocked areas and remove as I would do if the animal was physically standing in front of me. You can ask your pendulum to show you the direction for 'yes' and the corresponding direction for 'no'. In my case it is usually clockwise to affirm a question and anti-clockwise for no. Pendulums can come in many different forms, metal, wooden or crystal; it is a matter of personal taste. I love to work with the crystal ones as the crystals contain extra healing qualities that help with the healing processes. Though, as with all crystals used in healing work, it is important to cleanse them.

CHAPTER 9

Distant Healing and Readings from Hair Samples

If clients are geographically too far away for me to visit, either in the UK or in other countries, I ask owners to send a photograph and a hair or fur sample. From the energy of the samples and photographs, I can intuit a lot about what is going on for the animal, but even more amazingly, the animal can tell me a lot about its owner. This can relate to general health and well being, emotionally and physically, family matters, negative and spirit energies in the house and, of course, past life connections as with Vivienne and Sasha, described below. I never cease to be amazed at the information an animal can give about their owners, even down to injuries that occurred in childhood or certainly long before the animal came into their care.

Sasha the Lhasa Apso

This case illustrates how an animal has chosen to reincarnate in different forms.

I received a letter from Vivienne containing a small tuft of fluff and a cute picture of her charming Lhasa Apso dog Sasha. On the surface this little dog looked every inch a cuddly lap lying pooch. Boy was I wrong!

When holding the small sample of hair and studying the photograph, a flood of emotion poured through me. I then received visions of Tibetan monks fleeing a tyrannous regime. I felt that Sasha's present owner was one of the monks and Sasha was another. The two monks seemed very close and when Sasha's owner was severely injured, Sasha in this previous life as a monk, cared for him until the end, when he succumbed to his injuries. The two seemed to have a karmic contract to reunite in this life, so that Vivienne, the monk who had died and had been lovingly cared for, could repay Sasha's kindness, by incarnating as a gentle human that could lovingly tend to all Sasha's needs. What better way to be pampered than being an adored little dog that had all the love she could wish for showered upon her. When Vivienne received my report, amazingly, she was not surprised in the least. She admitted to a fascination with Buddhist philosophies and had always felt that their relationship was very special, but had not realized just how special!

Cindy's Connection

Kate sent me some photos and a fur sample of her cat Cindy. She wanted to know if they had had any past lives together as they seemed practically inseparable. They were so deeply connected. As I held the fur in my hand and studied the photo, Cindy immediately started to give me information of a very sensitive nature connected to female health, relating to Kate. I wondered how I was going to relay this information as it pertained to relationships and matters of intimacy. This was a surprise and I was puzzled as to where all this would lead. The information was so clear and it felt very important. I didn't want to embarrass Kate, so I knew I would have to be extremely careful as to how I would report my findings. Cindy gave me very clear information about physical conditions, which Kate verified later as absolutely correct.

Cindy then showed me a time when she was a temple cat and Kate was a priestess. This was a time when making love to a priestess was a sacred act and was supposed to give men extra powers, but as the priestesses grew in political strength and respect, male counterparts felt threatened and eventually the priestesses were disbanded and branded as whores, many were thrown out of the temples or even killed. The treatment that Kate received and the way she was abandoned by her temple left deep emotional scars that were still carried in her subconscious today.

Cindy seemed to know how limiting these negative self-beliefs were and how they were in danger of spoiling Kate's wonderful relationship with her partner. I emailed Kate, explaining that the reading had thrown up some quite sensitive information about her and asked if she would agree to a telephone conversation to discuss what Cindy had told me. Kate agreed, reassuring me that even though the information was of a personal nature she really wanted to know what the cat had to say. So I relayed all that Cindy had told me, gently describing the physical details, which Kate confirmed were true. I then went on to describe their past life together and Cindy's concerns that this was preventing Kate from being truly happy in her present life. Though Kate was obviously shocked that her little cat should know so much about her personal life, she agreed that there were some issues which needed addressing. The most important issue was that she and her partner desperately wanted a child and even though there seemed to be no physical reason that Kate could not conceive, they were having no luck and the pressure was beginning to tell on their relationship.

Thanks to Cindy's past life revelations, Kate was able to understand where her feelings about herself came from and she was able to let go of the past and start to enjoy the present. Only a few weeks later I received another email from Kate but this time there was a different kind of picture attached... a printout of a scan of their tiny baby in the womb. Kate assured me that everyone, human and feline, were overjoyed and looking forward in anticipation of the happy event, and more photos arrived a few months later.

Barking Fly

I had an SOS from a lady who owned a collie called Fly. She sent the usual hair sample and photo, but she was at her wit's end. Fly would not stop barking at her teenage daughter. If she saw the girl through the window coming home, Fly would throw herself at the glass in frenzy. The mother was also having problems with the girl and though teenagers can often display challenging behaviour, it seemed to be becoming more and more extreme. Fly's behaviour was becoming so bad that they thought the only kind thing to do was to either re-home her or put her to sleep.

Fly showed me that there was much tension in the home and frequent arguments, but she also said that the girl was being bullied by two girls at school. She went on to describe the girls in great detail, rather like the case of Chippy and Cara. However, when I relayed this information to the mother, she said that was rubbish as her daughter would have told her if she was being bullied. I said that I was only reporting what the dog had told me and I could only give the information I received. I was disappointed as I felt sure Fly was only trying to help in her rather disruptive way, but I guess she didn't know how else to alert the family to the problems and drastic measures had to be taken even if it risked her home and perhaps her life. The next day I received a phone call from Fly's owner. She apologised for being rather abrupt and said she had asked her daughter if she was being bullied and if it was the reason for her challenging behaviour. She told me her daughter had verified everything that Fly had said, even down to the description of the two girls, which were incredibly accurate.

I was so glad for Fly's sake, as she was only acting so badly out of desperation as she could not make her owners understand. They promptly contacted the school and the problem was addressed. I heard that Fly was much calmer and things were being resolved in the home, which, happily, was a much more peaceful environment to live in.

Butterfly the Rabbit

I had a letter from a lovely woman who adored her rabbits. She sent me several photos of her bunnies, but one in particular was very special and had no fur attached. This was because the rabbit had died and her lovely owner was desperate to see if I could communicate with the rabbit to see how she was. The rabbit was called Butterfly.

I had never attempted a reading for a rabbit before, much less a spirit one, but I said I would do my best. As I gazed at the photograph, I felt the most wonderful feelings of love come through me and I picked up my pen and started to write.

Butterfly was giving me all sorts of information about her owner's health and the welfare of other rabbits she was now caring for. One in particular was causing Butterfly some concern. She said that this rabbit was not eating the right food and that it was having some digestive troubles. Butterfly suggested a better diet and went on to discuss all sorts of other matters relating to the living rabbits' welfare. I was amazed at how thick and fast the information flowed from this wise little bunny.

Even more amazing was the feedback on receiving Butterfly's words of wisdom. Apparently all the recommendations that she had made for the sick rabbit had been suggested by their vet and Butterfly's owner was about to commence the new regime.

We were both astounded at this little rabbit's wisdom from spirit.

Butterfly went on to say that she was very busy, but another of the owner's favourite rabbits would be coming back to her very soon and Butterfly described what this rabbit would look like and she said that her owner would know exactly who it was.

I sincerely hope this lovely caring owner will be reunited with her beloved pet and that Butterfly will find time to return when she was not too busy watching over everyone.

Buddy, Sadie and Willie – the Soul Family
I did a reading for a Canadian couple called Janice and Ron that I'd met whilst working with humpback whales in the Dominican

119

Republic and again in Mexico when we swam with whale sharks. I have performed many many readings, but this one was so special, as each animal was such an integral part of the family and they had reconnected and reunited to form their soul family once again. I truly believe that our animals find us for this very reason. This reading completely confirmed this for me.

Janice was very curious about my work and felt she might like to have a reading for her animals to make sure they were happy and that their needs were being met. She didn't tell me anything about them, just their names and species. She obviously cared deeply for any animal and had a true compassion for all living things and the planet. Ron, I think, simply thought I was a little mad. So when I received a large package with photographs, fur and feathers, I was happy to get to work to see if I could help and I was truly amazed at this very special family. It was so amazing as the whole family – human and animal, were totally intertwined karmically, even down to Willy the dear little love bird. I had never before performed a reading whilst holding a feather, but it didn't seem to make any difference. I felt him chatting away to me over the miles from their home near Toronto.

Buddy is a gorgeous grey Manx cat with the most stunning piercing yellow eyes, which seemed to bore into my soul as I studied his picture. Sadie is a black Labrador cross. Her energy was so gentle and full of love and compassion for her owners.

I opened the envelope and saw the picture of Buddy first, and as soon as I looked into his eyes I thought 'Wow! What an extra-ordinary little being'. I felt like I was being given a history lesson from Buddy, who was showing me their Egyptian life in glorious Technicolor. The images he was giving me were so clear; it was as though I was experiencing all the sights, sounds, smells, textures and emotions of that ancient time. It was really interesting to observe the dynamics between Janice and Ron in the Ancient Egyptian lifetime that seems to have spilled over into the relationship today as a married couple. It is interesting to read the owner's feedback, verifying most of what the animals told me.

Madeleine's reading for Buddy the Manx cat:

I just love the photo of Buddy asleep. It's wonderful to realise that our animals truly find us instead of us choosing them.

Janice feedback: Yes, I know that Buddy found me. I was going through such a difficult time with my first cat, Bunny, slowly dying over a number of months. I was doing everything I could for her to keep her going. But the time finally came for me to put her down. She just wouldn't go of her own accord. We learned of Buddy about a week or so before I had to put Bunny down. And

exactly one week after she was gone, I picked up Buddy to take him home with me. My sister (who is also our vet!) introduced me to Buddy as he came in as a stray into her clinic by strangers who found him injured on the side of the road. He was hurt badly and had potential

Buddy

health issues that my sister discovered by running tests. These strangers were good Samaritans to bring him in and had no connections to this cat. And of all the vet clinics – he ended up at my sister's! Debbie saw he was a very special cat and introduced me to him. I can't thank her enough. She helped him to recover from his injuries.

Madeleine's reading: Buddy found you when he strayed because he needed to bring this balance and gentle strength to you, to help your healing work. I know that you may not overtly be healing, but in providing solutions for people and caring so deeply for animals, you are channelling your healing abilities.

Janice feedback: Buddy came into my life at a time when my first cat was in her dying days. Hers was a slow decline over many months and Buddy showed up in her final days of life. She was also a Manx, so when Buddy arrived as a stray and was also a Manx, and in need of a home, I knew it was meant to be for me to adopt him. What are the chances of another Manx cat walking into your life as the other one is exiting?

You are correct. I am not "out there" visibly healing; however, I do in my own little ways, try to make the world a better place. I do try to help people with their pet or animal problems/issues by providing information and solutions for them. As well – since I spend a lot of time in my car, I am always scanning the roads when I drive to "save" animals from their dangers. Just on Saturday I had to drive into the city and I helped a turtle cross the road on my way in. And on my way back home I helped another turtle cross the road. For sure these two turtles would have had a dangerous time trying to cross. I was so happy to have had the opportunity to save their lives. I see more dead turtles than live turtles on the roads and my heart sinks each time I see one that didn't make it. Why don't more people just take the minute it takes to pull over and help any of these creatures cross safely? I've also helped countless other animals (snakes, frogs, toads, birds, snails, possum, raccoons, porcupine, and caterpillars) be safe. You have to help those who cannot help themselves. And my pets are all "rescues". I assume this is just another way to help heal the earth, whenever I see road-kill, I bless those creatures and pray they are at peace now and in a better place. As it is too late for me to do anything to help them now physically, I bless them and send them love. That is all I can do for them now.

Madeleine's reading: He's such a wise cat – it's almost like you live with him rather than he lives with you!

Janice feedback: Yes, he is very intelligent. He seems to have so much wisdom, boldness, and confidence about him. Much of the time Buddy seems to be running the show.

Madeleine's reading: He's showing me some dark brown diamond or triangular shaped treats that he likes (coming back to the mundane again now) and says he loves fish.

Janice feedback: Yes, he loves fish. I know these treats you are referring to. They are actually treats I bought for Sadie which are dark brown and square and flat in shape. They are very chewy. Buddy gets a little corner off these treats, so the shape of the treat I give to Buddy is actually triangular.

Madeleine's reading: He says he loves his sheepskin bed and loves luxury – he does not like to 'rough it'.

Janice feedback: Yes – Buddy does have a sheepskin-type bed and enjoys it and he does love the luxury of being pampered. He is in no hurry to "escape" the house. He is an indoor cat now and we are very careful at watching that he cannot get out. He never tries that hard though.

Madeleine's reading: He is very good at helping you both unwind as he'll just cuddle up or do something funny to help you 'lighten up' – he's really good at stopping you taking life too seriously.

Janice feedback: Yes – you are absolutely correct!

Madeleine's reading: He says he left his old home because there was too much shouting and there was a large brown dog that chased him and really frightened him. I get the feeling that he really doesn't like raised voices now and will make himself scarce if you have loud visitors – I can see him welcoming people that he likes, but he's very discerning.

Janice feedback: We do not know his background so I have no way of confirming this. Yes, he does welcome people into the house and he also bids them farewell. We joke amongst ourselves that he is more like a dog, than like a cat, in this way – running to the front door when the bell rings and meeting people coming through the door. Too funny.

Madeleine's reading for Sadie:

Sadie's a really gorgeous dog. She is incredibly loving and loyal. She's showing me possums and racoons – have you had a problem with racoons? She's showing me that she's been barking at some undergrowth. She loves life and adores being in the great outdoors with you both.

Janice feedback: Sadie is incredibly loyal and loving, especially with me. She has me in her sights all the time. She follows me everywhere I go. I call her my "little shadow". We regularly have raccoons visit in the backyard. The raccoons eat the birdseed that has fallen from the feeders. Sadie looks out for the raccoons every evening. She will sit at the back window and wait and look. She seems so interested in them. We live out in the country in the woods, so yes – this is definitely the great outdoors. Sadie very much enjoys being outside. Sometimes she doesn't want to come inside at the end of the day.

Madeleine's reading: Sadie's showing me some rubber boots (we call them wellies). She says she loves to 'help' in the garden and feels really excited when either you or Ron put these boots on!

Janice feedback: Absolutely! Ron and I each own a pair of these rubber boots and we putter around the yard and gardens with these on. When Sadie sees us put on the boots she gets excited because she knows this means outdoor activities are forthcoming. She follows me everywhere I go.

Madeleine's reading: She says she doesn't really like the vacuum cleaner and prefers it when you sweep the floor. I think she quite likes to play with the brush (maybe when she was younger?) She says she's sorry about all the hairs but some are Buddy's!

Janice feedback: Sadie must hear me complaining about all the dog hair! I see her hair mostly on the floor and this is mainly the hair that I complain about. Yes – Sadie absolutely hates the vacuum cleaner. We figure it is the loud noise it makes. Sadie seems sensitive to loud sounds. Every time we vacuum she runs around the house trying to get away from it. We try to vacuum when she is outside.

Madeleine's reading: She is also making me hear wind chimes and something in the house connected to Tibet?

Janice feedback: Yes, we do have wind chimes outside. One is in the backyard where we feed the birds, and the squirrels, chipmunks and raccoons. Sometimes, when they are feeding you can hear the chimes because they are being jostled. The only thing in the house which may sound Tibetan would be an old wall clock that we have. It chimes every hour and every half hour.

Madeleine's reading: Sadie is such a wise dog and it's almost as if she and Buddy are a double act. She has deep Egyptian connections with you and Buddy. I can see Sadie as a pharaoh hound – the more I look at her photo the more she turns into Anubis! He was god of the underworld but was a very positive, balancing, levelling sort of energy.

They are deeply connected karmically and know what the other is doing the whole time as they communicate telepathically constantly. They also know both of your moods before you even get home and before you wake up and are great listeners if you have the blues about anything. It's quite difficult to separate Sadie from Buddy as their energies are so entwined.

Janice feedback: Buddy and Sadie definitely do have an understanding and a friendly, loving relationship between them. When Sadie shares her food or bed with Buddy, you know there must be some sort of communication and understanding or relationship between the two. There has never been any hostility between them.

Madeleine's reading: She seems very self-contained whilst you are at work - just communicating with Buddy and feels very happy and secure in her 'family'.

Janice feedback: Yes Madeleine, you are absolutely correct – I know this to be true. A few years back I was taking Sadie to doggy day care once or twice a week, and although they took very good care of her there and she had plenty of fun and exercise and long walks out in the countryside (she always slept so soundly each evening after spending the day there, she was exhausted from all the days activities) – I just knew in my heart that she'd rather stay at home while Ron and I were away at work for the day. She'd seem apprehensive when I would drop her off in the morning and I sensed that she didn't like to see me turn my back on her and walk away. If I gave her a choice she would want to jump back in the car with me than stay at the day care. If Sadie had absolutely loved it and looked forward to it, I was willing to pay for her to be there. But I got the feeling that Sadie was just as happy, or even happier, just to stay at home. So I figured Buddy and her can keep each other company.

Madeleine's reading: Did Sadie come from a home where they would have spoken French? because I can hear a French Canadian accent from her early puppy days.

Janice feedback: As we got Sadie from the local humane society as a stray, they had no history of her – neither do we. Sorry – cannot confirm this.

Madeleine's reading: I also get that she may have had a digestive problem by eating a foreign object or something that upset her.

Janice feedback: Yes, Sadie did have an intestinal/digestive problem. It was so bad at times that she was peeing blood and there was blood in her stools. We were quite concerned about her. Ron and I didn't know what was causing the problem. We figured she must have eaten something bad in the woods. She was treated by my sister (the vet) and Sadie did get better but then the problems reoccurred. We began to think that maybe her issues were related to the food she was eating, maybe it was too rich for her or maybe she developed some sort of allergy to it? We switched her food over to another type which was specific for dogs with sensitive stomachs. This worked. Since we put her on this new food she has had no further problems. This all happened less than a year ago.

Madeleine's reading: She's telling me about a knee problem (with Ron I think), did he play ice hockey when he was younger? I feel there's a sports injury there somewhere. I'm getting a possible cartilage injury?

Janice feedback: I am the one with the knee injury. I've had problems with my right knee since October 2004. Ron and I were at the Toronto airport, just returning from a trip to the United States and I sprained my knee by stepping off the curb while picking up my suitcase. This must have put too much strain on the knee and it just snapped. It took a very, very long time for it to get better and it is still not 100 per cent.

I was going for massage therapy, physiotherapy and I even had an MRI scan done on it because it was taking so long to heal. If I exert my knee now in any way it starts to give me problems with swelling, stiffness and soreness. At the time you did this reading I was gardening quite a bit around the house, digging, which aggravated my knee and it was hurting me again.

Madeleine's reading: I also feel that Sadie might get a slight problem with her hips as she gets older, but nothing too serious.

Janice feedback: I too think Sadie may experience hip problems as she gets older. Many breeds of larger sized dogs do experience hip problems (displasia) and I feel that Sadie may be susceptible to this as well. She has a long spine and she is considered a large dog so I am a little concerned about this for her. I address this potential health problem now by feeding her small daily doses of glucosamine and chondroitin complex. These compounds are good for the wellbeing of the joints. I am also taking this complex in the form of pills to help my knee heal. So that is why I feed Sadie these particular doggy treats called Hipaction. They are glucosamine and chondroitin fortified treats for dogs – and the flavour I give her (which she absolutely loves and Buddy too!) is Beef Formula.

Madeleine's reading for Willie: What a pretty chap – again very sensitive to what's going on. He's telling me that his previous home was not as nice as this one and he was not treated as well – he's saying something about being kept in the dark more.

Janice feedback: Willie's previous home was a temporary one. The people were taking care of him, basically fostering Willie, until Willie's real owner got his life back together. Willie's real owner was going through some major life changes, divorce, moving, job changes, and he was not able to keep Willie at the time with so much turmoil. So, this fellow's mom stepped up to the plate and said she would take care of Willie until her son was ready to have Willie back. Well, about two long years went by and Willie was still in the care of the mom. He was kept in the basement at her house because she owned a cat and two Jack Russell dogs and all these critters wanted to do was to harm Willie. So Willie was kept in the basement for his own safety. I know the mom did the best she could for Willie to make him comfortable; however, she knew a basement was no place for a bird. I had hinted to this family that if they ever were going to find this bird a new home to keep me in mind. I remember seeing him in the basement and I was so upset and sad to know that this was where he was spending his time. So when the time arrived that the son finally decided he no longer had room in his life for this bird, I was approached by the mom and Willie was given to me. Willie is always kept in bright rooms now that he is with us. He has plenty of exposure sunshine too. On those beautiful, warm summer days, he is outside in his cage from morning to evening. He does rather enjoy it. We have bird feeders outside and he can view the wild birds and chirp back and forth with them.

Madeleine's reading: He's telling me either you or Ron gets a stiff neck and shoulders from computer work and sometimes this leads to headaches. He says he can feel your aches in his head and you need to do gentle neck rolls, like he does!

Janice feedback: I am the one that gets a stiff neck and shoulders from all the computer use at work. I sit at the computer all day hardly taking any breaks most days. It was so awful within the last two years or so, I was actually going for massage therapy as well as physiotherapy for months and months and months to help relieve the aches and pains. I had to make several adjustments to my computer work station, mouse and keyboard at work to help relieve the repetitious strain of the job on my body. All the computer work has also been giving me headaches because of severe eye strain. I have visited both my doctor and my optometrist many times within the last year looking to relieve the severe discomfort I feel in my eyes when working on the computer. When the strain is severe my head will ache. I will take Willie's advice and do the gentle neck rolls!

Madeleine's reading: I'm getting that there may have been a problem with his beak in the past and he didn't like being handled – he's showing me someone having to trim it or something and he wasn't impressed!

Janice feedback: I am not aware of any beak issues since Willie joined us. You did say you got a feeling that this was in the past. I will need to ask the previous owner about this.

Madeleine's reading: He has taken it upon himself to entertain you and brighten up your life after a hard day – he will just lift your mood with his colourful personality and vibrant plumage.

He says he likes his freedom to fly, but also likes the security of his cage. He doesn't mind being on his own because he chats to Sadie and Buddy.

Janice feedback: We let Willie out of the cage to fly about every day. At certain times he is really eager to get out. Other times he is content to sit in his cage and eat, preen himself, or just sit there comfortable and look out at the world. I know he does like the security and safety of his cage – you can tell. When Ron and I leave the house to go to work, Willie (in his cage) is placed in a room upstairs with the door closed for his safety. We do not trust Buddy 100% to be alone with the bird, seeing that he is a cat! Buddy does not attempt to harm Willie. It is like he knows Willie is a part of the family and not to be treated as a potential meal. However we think it is better to be safe than sorry. I've often thought poor Willie is all alone upstairs, but maybe he is not so alone after all if they are all communicating in the house even though they are not all together in the same room.

Madeleine's reading: He's showing me some orange coloured drinking water. Has he had some sort of treatment given in his water? He says he likes grapes and he's also showing little pieces of red apple.

Janice feedback: I am normally very good at changing Willie's drinking water so it is fresh for him – if not every day, it is changed every second day. Madeleine, about the time you did his reading, I had not changed Willie's water for three days. I didn't get it changed until the third day (oops – sorry Willie!!!) and I noticed that his water, which is normally clear, was orange coloured. I felt so bad – poor little guy didn't have fresh drinking water. Some weeks ago I ran out of his regular food, this has no coloured seeds in it. So currently his diet consists of this food which has coloured pieces in it.

I remember I had grapes in the house over the weekend and I was eating some. Willie was loose in the house and landed on my shoulder. He seemed interested so I let Willie taste it. He liked it! He kept biting into it and he seemed to be eating it as well – not just tasting it. This impressed upon me because I try different fresh fruits and vegetables on him and for the most part I do not think he is that impressed with fresh food. I think this must be due to his upbringing; he probably wasn't exposed to or fed much of this fresh food at all when he was growing up. I just couldn't get over how much Willie seemed to enjoy that grape! I actually decided to keep the grape for him so he could have some later – I left the half a piece of grape on the kitchen counter. When I let Ron read the printout of your readings, he made a question/comment about Willie liking grapes. I had to show Ron the grape I saved for Willie because he seemed to like it so much the day before. Isn't that something! I think you made an impression on Ron – and that's difficult to do! I keep telling him there is more to the world than what meets the eye!

Madeleine's reading: I feel that you are all connected and have all been together before – even Willy who has Osiris (falcon energy)! Sadie is showing me that in your past lives, you and Ken were priests in Egypt, with a deep compassion for all things, but there was a deep inner conflict to feel compassion to injustices, which I know will outrage you in this present life. It was at this time when all the old gods and beliefs were being smashed by Akhenaton who brought in the new regimes of worshiping just one god. Buddy's giving me a history lesson in glorious Technicolor! He is showing me so much destruction of sacred places as Akhenaton's ego consumed him, especially when Nefertiti died – he seemed to lose it completely. Buddy was a temple cat in your Egyptian life and was very much revered. I'm getting that Willie was one of the Pharaoh's falcons that you were in charge of. It was one of your tasks to tend to the royal falcons that possessed the spirit of Osiris.

At first it felt as though all would be well and there would be a gentle shift into the new way of thinking, but there was so much anger and jealousy. I feel that Ron loved the temple life, with its gentle existence. You found it very hard to accept new regimes and changes that were quite destructive. I can feel that this spills out in your present day work. Sadie is telling me that because of your strong views you were persecuted by the new regimes and beliefs that were being implemented by people that did not agree with your ethos. I feel that Sadie and Buddy were with you then in different guises, but very aware of the situation. It feels like Ron tried to keep the peace, but admired your courage – he was just fearful of where it might lead you. In some ways he wished he could be more like you, but tried to do his own bit in a more covert way. This feels as though there is a connection in this life, where you balance each other and all this time the animals are monitoring the two of you.

Janice feedback: I will have to look into this Egyptian history... I am not very familiar with it. What you are saying does sound intriguing though.

Madeleine's reading: It's like Sadie and Buddy have taken it upon themselves to reincarnate at this time to help you get in touch with your gentle healer self.

CHAPTER 10

Learning to Listen – Can Anyone Do This?

When working intuitively with animals and people, you can experience such a range and rollercoaster of emotions, ranging from the hilarious to the tragic. All must be treated with the utmost honour and respect. Everyone who is open to the concept of telepathic communication can learn to communicate with every living thing on the planet – and possibly the spirits of those who have died too. It's simply a question of remembering our long buried skills. It only depends on how committed you are to deepening your connection to all that is. How prepared are you to delve into yourself?

A Message from a Fly

When opening up to communing with the beauty of the universe you have to become aware of the beauty or Divine within. I had a pertinent lesson in this from a common fly! Flies can have very important messages for us. When I recounted this story to workshop participants, they said that from then on they would feel very differently towards flies and try to refrain from the instinctive swatting reaction that we all seem to do, when a fly dares to land on us.

I was sitting in the garden enjoying some wonderful spring sunshine, when a fly landed on my arm. I was just about to swish it away when I stopped short and suddenly felt as if the fly was fixing me with a very steady and important stare! I began to hear a very important message about myself, coming from this tiny creature. Its wise words were: "You give so much love to everybody and everything else, why don't you open your heart and let **yourself** in!"

I had to admit I was quite shocked at such a profound statement coming from such an unexpected source. However I could easily see the truth in the words. I had been feeling quite isolated and had always been my own worst critic. I know that to truly love others you have to love yourself, so I promised to work on this challenge and thanked the fly for its willingness to help. It seemed to nod in satisfaction and then buzzed off.

Learning to listen is the first part; really hearing is the important bit. It was not enough to just be aware of the message that the fly gave me, I had to really **hear** its meaning and act on it. Working to open our hearts is the best way to create channels of communication. There are different ways of intuiting information, none are better than others. It is important to value and not dismiss the way in which your intuitive skills develop. You may work using just one of the following techniques or a mixture, each is just as valid.

Extrasensory Perceptions
Different Ways of Connecting with Animals

Clairvoyance
This literally means "clear seeing". This refers to the ability to see images and pictures in your mind's eye. It refers to the ability to intuitively know something about the past, present, or future without any logical explanation as to why you would know it. This refers to the 'video clip' type images that I can intuit of past or present lives. I sometimes get shown how an animal will appear in the future when it next incarnates. I have been shown very clearly how a beloved goat companion of mine called Anneka, will reincarnate. She told me quite vehemently, from spirit, that she would not return as another goat as she didn't want to live in a cold stable. She is coming back to me in the form of a cat so she can curl up on my bed or snuggle in my lap! I can totally believe this of her as she always followed me wherever I

went and was incredibly in tune with me. I lost her one day and knew she would not be far away but I was not quite prepared for where I would find her. She was in my bedroom! We lived in a bungalow and wanting to be near me she had pushed open our kitchen stable door and discovered the delights of our home. She made no mess, but had found a collage of a greenfinch that my eldest son Christopher had lovingly made at playschool. It was made from various seeds and Anneka thought she would sample a few. She looked very at home picking the seeds off the paper, desecrating the picture. She obviously remembered that bedrooms were good places to find oneself in!

Clairsentience

This means "clear feeling" and it refers to the ability to feel the emotions or physical feelings of another intuitively. Sometimes you can begin to feel pain or anxiety in your body that you know isn't yours. Care must be taken to let go of this and not take on the person's or animal's condition. Imagining sending everything down to be grounded is a good way of clearing yourself. When working on remote readings I often feel a physical pain or a heaviness of heart, which helps me intuit problems with the person or understand what the animal is showing me about itself or its owner.

Clairaudience

This means "clear hearing". This refers to the ability to hear words and phrases in your mind's ear. This is also known as mental telepathy. When you hear this way, the words and phrases may sound like your own voice, but if your information can be verified, you can learn to trust your abilities. Trust is the all important word. Sometimes although the sound of the voice is the same, the tone is very different from each animal. I once worked with five dogs that lived in a house with their owner. Each dog had a very individual character and distinctive energy which was reflected in the tone of its communication. They liked to gossip about each other, which was very amusing and proved correct when verifying with the owner. One dog was very quiet and self contained, so it communicated in a steady and sensible way. Another was completely hyperactive so spoke really quickly and rattled on about all sorts of antics that the others had been getting up to. I once talked with a lovely mare called Moonie and her tone was one that I imagine an agony aunt would sound like. She was commenting on her owner's boyfriend saying that he really wasn't good enough for her and she could do so much better. I had to try not to laugh as it was such an endearing but authoritative tone. Ironically, the owner's mother was attending the session. I tactfully tried to relay the horse's thoughts on the relationship, with which she heartily agreed. I'm glad to say that the owner was coming to the same conclusion.

Clairalience

This means "clear smelling". This is an ability that is less common, but some people get very clear impressions of smells, sometimes associated with a loved one from the past (for example, a perfume), sometimes with a distinct message for the present. Animals sometimes give me smells to describe their likes and dislikes. This can be of food or an environment. Cats and dogs regularly give me meaty smells, which isn't very pleasant when you're vegetarian, but they love it. Horses can sometimes give me the smell of molasses or apples which can then spill over into the next category.

Clairhambience

This means "clear tasting" and it is the intuitive ability to get impressions of taste. An example would be asking a cat to tell you her favourite food and getting an impression of the taste of fish. A dog that attended one of my workshops as a willing helper for us to work on caused much hilarity when we asked her what her favourite food was (always a good place to start when communicating with animals). I smelt and tasted fish and she showed me a little symbol of a fish. I thought I had the correct answer, but one of my students knew better. She intuited that the dog loved fish cakes.

We all laughed until the owner confirmed that this dog was passionate about fish cakes. It was a big lesson in trusting guidance for that student as even she thought what she was being told must be nonsense. Who ever heard of a dog loving fishcakes? This one did!

Too Many Chips

Tact is a very important skill to develop. We have a huge responsibility in how we convey messages and it is our duty to relay information with the utmost integrity. However this is not always easy, as some messages are quite personal and could cause offence. A great example of this was when I was working on a very well bred and expensive show pony, one of several on the yard. The owner had called me in because she was worrying about various problems that the ponies were displaying, physically and emotionally. I was amazed to be told, amongst other gossip about the ponies, that the owner was eating too many chips or French fries! Far from being derogatory the pony was only concerned with the owner's health, not her weight. She was a very slim lady so I felt disinclined to tell her the message from the pony. However, the pony insisted that I tell her. When I summoned up the courage to repeat the pony's statement, the owner roared with laughter, thankfully, and proceeded to tell me the truth of the matter. In order to supplement her finances that were stretched by having to pay for all the ponies, she had started work in a local pub serving meals in the evening. She had indeed been eating chips and had gained several pounds in the last month. I reassured her that the pony only had her best interests at heart and was not referring to obesity just the fat content.

Angry Toast

Another amusing and slightly tricky occasion was when I was working with a rescue cob called William. His new owner was devoted to him and he was very lucky to find himself in such a good home, no doubt for a very good reason in order to bring enlightenment to his owner. He showed me his owner making toast for someone I assumed was her husband. He showed me two slices of white toast being prepared. However, this was not being done with very good grace; I had the strong impression that the owner was very grumpy with her partner. William insisted that I found a way of relating this. Luckily for me the owner found it highly amusing and admitted that she had been very cross with her husband because she felt he had not been pulling his weight and she had indeed given him two slices of white toast. This had happened that very morning, just before she had met me for our session with William. William suggested that she needed to be less stressed and calmer as he said she could be moody. The owner admitted this was true and we laughed that perhaps she should take a new equine supplement designed for troublesome, hormonal mares. The owner said that she would tell her husband, who had been very sceptical about my visit and felt that he would now have a very positive reaction to my information.

Henry's Cream Cakes

Another funny episode was when I visited a large bay horse called Henry. Amongst many other pieces of information relating to his condition, he started to show me pictures of pasta and scrumptious cream cakes. I had groaned inwardly thinking, "Here we go again!" as Henry said I had to tell his owner this vital message. This was a lesson in not doubting yourself, which I still sometimes do when the information seems so bizarre. I forced myself to mention the culinary delights, much to the surprise of the owner. She admitted that pasta was her favourite food and she would quite happily exist totally on a diet of pasta. About the cream cakes, she was not so sure. She did admit to an occasional indulgence, but not an obsession. So we returned to more profound exchanges which I hoped would benefit them both. I dismissed the cream cakes as being irrelevant. However, when I returned home from my long journey from Henry's yard, I received a text from his owner saying that when she returned home from our session she had opened the fridge and inside were two cream cakes her husband had bought as a special treat.

The Music Buff Budgie

When I visited Chippy the cat and worked with his young lady friend Cara, her younger brother asked me if I could chat to his budgie. I had never talked to a budgerigar before but thought I would give it a try as I didn't want to disappoint the young fellow. I opened the door of the bedroom containing the bird cage, carefully closing it behind me because of Chippy. I didn't want any disasters where the cat obtained an extra feathery meal. I was met by a very disgruntled bird that stomped up and down his perch looking very cross. I asked him if it was ok to approach and talk and he grudgingly acquiesced. He demanded that I do something about the terrible music. The radio was left playing in his room to give the bird some company whilst the children were at school. The bird's feathered companion had recently died and they were worried he might be lonely. The radio was tuned into a local station playing pop music. The budgie was not amused and detested what he described as a 'racket'. It reminded me of my Grandfather's similar feelings on the subject which he described as a 'cascade of cacophony'. I was slightly shocked at this little bird's vehemence. I promised I would take it up with the management. Naturally they were slightly bemused by my questions regarding the radio, but admitted to recently changing the station from classical music to this playing more modern tunes. When I said that the budgie strongly objected to being inflicted with this music they promised to tune into some 'proper music'! I was glad to hear that the budgie was much happier and was chatting away happily to the classical compositions.

Harry's Swear Box

Not all dialogue from animals is repeatable. I was shocked to enter a barn one day. Only to hear the foulest language coming from a horse called Harry. I had no idea that horses could swear and if this horse had a swear box he would soon be bankrupt.

When I asked permission to enter his stable, I was met with a tirade of abuse. Words to the effect of what on earth did I think I could do to help? He obviously had a very poor regard for humans, for which I had to apologise. He told me that he was pulled up in a race when he could have won and was so angry as he felt that he had given his all and was now discarded, lame and depressed. I tried to reassure him that I would do what I could to make things better for him. He had come to the yard to convalesce and his future was by no means secure. Fortunately the people caring for him were very understanding and really wanted him to remain in their care and if he became sound again they would race him, but only if he wanted to. He had tendon problems in a foreleg that had been very painful. He said that he would like to race again but this time with a lady jockey and on a specific type of course, only on his terms.

I relayed his requests as promised and when we had finished his session he said in my head, "My leg feels better but don't tell them that!" Luckily for Harry, he was able to stay at that home and he began to be fit enough to race. According to his needs, a lady jockey was booked for the race and off he went. I waited to hear the outcome with baited breath. Later on that evening I received a phone call to say that Harry had been triumphant and had won his race easily. When I next saw him I congratulated him. He was bending over his stable door imploring the little children who were cycling past to come a bit closer so he could bite them. He was quite a character and his language hadn't improved much. I suppose old habits die hard!

Jazz's Anger

The only horse I have felt truly threatened by was a huge show jumper mare called Jazz. She was so full of anger and rage that I was really scared to be near her. In fact, she recommended that I leave her stable as she would not be responsible for her actions. I believed her and speedily vacated her space. I tried to reassure her that I had come to help and asked what she could tell me about her anger. From the safety of the other side of her stable door, she began to tell me what had enraged her.

She had been at livery in a show jumping yard where she also received some schooling over fences. Sadly some show jumping trainers still use unscrupulous methods to get horses to jump. There are many wonderful trainers and yards but unfortunately this was not one of them. Jazz told me that there was some very cruel treatment to some of the horses, which caused bad injuries to their legs. Her owner had noticed some sore places on Jazz and had complained strongly, so luckily Jazz fared better than many of the other horses in the yard. She told me of her best friend was a chestnut that had experienced very harsh treatment. Jazz could not understand why she had been left in this awful place and was so furious at the stupidity and insensitivity of the human race. Her poor owner was heartbroken when I told her what Jazz was saying to me. She had desperately wanted to move Jazz, but couldn't find another yard near enough to take her and she was trying to cope with terrible family illness. Jazz went on to tell me some very disturbing facts about the manager of the yard who was a very hard woman. Jazz told me that she had suffered terrible abuse when she was a child which had left her emotionally scarred and having to prove her dominance at all cost. The owner was quite shocked at what I had been told. She blurted, "How could you know that?" I told her that I didn't, but her horse had just told me. Apparently, recently someone who knew the yard manager's history had imparted her childhood history to Jazz's owner, which verified everything she had told me in graphic detail.

Billy and the Blitz

It never ceases to amaze me what animals know about us and our past history. They will tell me about a childhood injury of their owner or something that happened before the animal ever came to the owner, just to prove how in tune they are with us. Obviously if they were living with their owner at that time in another guise it proves how much they care about helping us release past trauma or self-limiting beliefs.

I was called out to meet Billy by his exasperated owners who were a lovely couple who had retired to Devon. Billy was a Jack Russell terrier and quite a character. The reason for his owner's difficulties was that he would not stop barking. Going in the car was a nightmare because his incessant noise was deafening. Any loud bangs or fireworks incensed him. He didn't seem frightened, just annoyed. Billy told me he was worried about the welfare and health of his owners who were not as fit as they used to be. He asked me to enquire about certain symptoms that would illustrate his awareness of their issues. He said that he was worried for their safety in the car and any anxiety that they had was heightened and intensified in Billy. He then said something very funny: "For goodness sake tell her to pick her feet up!" I tried not to laugh as I mentioned this to the lady of the house and she burst out laughing. Apparently she had made several stumbles whilst climbing their stairs and steps up into their home and had fallen several times, much to Billy's exasperation.

Things got very emotional when Billy went on to show me a small tan coloured cross-bred, terrier type, dog , struggling with the devastation of London in the war time blitz. He showed me a young girl holding this little dog who he said was called Sam. The awful drone of the bombs overhead and the terror they instilled in the families trying to survive at that time was relayed in my head. The little tan terrier had given much consolation to the little girl at that dreadful time. As I looked up from stroking Billy as he recounted all this, his owner had tears streaming down her face. She had been the little girl and she did indeed have a little tan dog called Sam at that time and he had been greatly mourned when he had died. Billy said that he had been Sam and that he had come back to look after his mistress and her husband in their later years. I felt he was still trying to protect them and the sound of fireworks and bangs reminded him of the blitz and he felt that some awful impending disaster would occur. He felt that he was unable to control and protect his owners in the car, so barked to remind them to be careful. Unfortunately this hindered more than it helped as the sound was so distracting. We discussed various remedies that might be useful to obtain from a holistic vet and I worked to release some of the fear that Billy had for his owners, making sure that they would be more careful to look after their health, for Billy's sake if not their own.

Ned the Shetland Scientist

I had been called out to see Julie and her horse Jack, who had been displaying some challenging behaviour and she had lost her confidence in riding him. We had a lovely session where Jack had described their past life together when Julie was a small boy working with heavy horses in the rail yards. Standing in the background was a diminutive skewbald Shetland pony, who I was told was called Ned. He seemed to be eavesdropping on our conversation and nodding wisely as if to say, "Well, I could have told you that". I worked with Julie and Jack helping to release their fears.

The past life information seemed to explain all the challenging behaviour and once it was understood it could be released. Ned seemed to have much more pressing information he wanted to impart. He pushed in between us and to my surprise he started to show me pictures of young children going into a playground of a typical village school. He showed me two little girls, both blonde, one had a ponytail and the other had plaits. He said they were good friends but he was a little concerned about them. I relayed this to Julie who looked a bit shocked because Ned had described her little girl, her best friend and their village school. How could Ned know this? Obviously he knew what Julie's daughter would look like and her friend might have come to play, but how could he describe the school in such precise detail? He went on to tell me that the daughter was going down with a nasty cough that had spread as a virus was doing the rounds at school. He then showed me a schoolroom with children sitting at small desks and a child coughing. He showed me what looked like lime green particles being sprayed out and becoming airborne into the atmosphere. Julie's daughter was then breathing in these green particles. To Ned's nonchalance, Julie admitted that there had been an awful cough going around the school and she suspected that her daughter was coming down with it.

Willing Teachers

This illustrates that we should never dismiss, underestimate or undervalue these wonderful creature's wisdom. It is a case of being open and being grateful to them for being willing to share their astounding knowledge with us. Their words of wisdom can be life changing for their owners. I always ask permission to work with animals. Before leaving to facilitate a workshop helping

students learn these skills, I always thank the animals in anticipation of their guidance and profound help. I am never disappointed at their willingness to instruct novice participants and the animals are always the stars of the show. They are the teachers; I am just a conduit

Rue

or a vehicle for the information to be relayed. I was particularly grateful to a tiny guinea pig called Rue who gave so much healing to Elsa, one of the participants of a workshop, who was experiencing difficult times in her life. When she entered the venue, I felt that her energy was out of balance and all was not well with her. This was a stage two workshop, so we discussed our experiences practicing communication and healing techniques that had been learnt from the previous workshop. Elsa mentioned several difficult changes had occurred in her life since our last meeting. As the day progressed, with the help of the animals, her energy lifted slightly, but she was still not her usual bubbly self. Until we met Dill and Rue, the two guinea pigs that happily joined our throng. We had been discussing the chakra systems and related emotional connotations. Elsa decided to try to communicate with Rue and gently cuddled her on her chest. The little cavy snuggled in to her and remained motionless for ten minutes. I was monitoring the group, and became aware that there was a wonderful healing taking place for Elsa. Her whole countenance had softened and her face looked serene. I instinctively knew that Rue was pouring healing energy into Elsa's heart chakra and was releasing her sadness and heaviness of heart. When the time came for a tea break, Elsa begrudgingly gave little Rue up to her young owners, and admitted to feeling so much lighter and happier. She couldn't believe how different she felt after her cuddle with the little furry healer.

Betty's Advice
Another wonderful horse called Betty gave advice and healing to every member of a workshop that I ran in Dorset. Hamish had admitted to being very nervous of horses and was not sure how he would cope working in close proximity with them during the encounters in the indoor arena working with horses. We had worked on various visualizations during the morning, connecting with power animals, creating balls of healing energy and had

practiced our fairly simple telepathic questions to the dogs that had come to help us. We asked questions like, what is your favourite food. Where do you like to sleep? Do you have a favourite place to visit or walk? What are your likes and dislikes? Is there anything you need to change in your life? Is there any thing you want to tell your human companion? We had enjoyed many stimulating answers, but nothing earth shatteringly profound, until we met Betty in the afternoon. Hamish had managed to connect to a lovely grey horse, but had kept his distance. When Betty was brought into the school, everything changed. She was a slender lithe chestnut mare and we discovered that although she was nearly five years old, she had spent the whole of her life living in a small herd in a large field. She had hardly been handled and had never really socialised. We visualized sending threads of loving energy from our hearts to connect with hers and asked with the deepest respect, if she might work with us. She gave us permission and we chatted about various topics telepathically. Most students were feeling that they were receiving answers to their questions. We 'heard' that she missed a dark bay friend and we learnt from her owner that she did indeed have a dark bay horse that had travelled with her, but it had been sold to another home, so they had been separated. Betty took this all in her stride and was very patient with the group's attempts at connecting with her. Suddenly she marched forwards. She had been standing quietly in the middle of our group's circle, but she made her advances to each and everyone of the group, whilst I translated what she was saying. This amazing horse approached Hamish so gently and talked about his fears and where they came from. Betty showed me a terrible death that Hamish had endured when he had been trampled by horses in a past life, which explained his inexplicable phobia. Nothing had ever happened in this lifetime to create his fear; he just felt acute physical and emotional discomfort. Betty suggested that Hamish should lie in a warm bath and visualize all his wounds and fears being washed away. By the time Betty had finished her dialogue, Hamish already seemed calmer and happier in her presence. When she was satisfied that she had helped Hamish, she then went on to discuss a lovely horse in spirit that caused much emotion with the student who had owned and adored it. Betty told the student that the horse was standing right behind her and was watching over her. She had to stop being so sad and acknowledge her spirit presence and guidance. Betty went on to discuss various health and emotional problems with the rest of the group and we were all left speechless at the wealth of knowledge this horse possessed. She had never even left her field until three weeks before, yet she seemed to be able to help the whole group in some relevant, specific way. It was quite astonishing. It gave Hamish the confidence to conquer his fears and begin working with all sorts of animals, including horses.

Maddy the Medium

Many horses can act as mediums and bring in loved ones who have passed. I worked with a horse called Maddy who brought in the spirit of her owner's grandmother and showed her baking cakes and making sweets as she said she wanted to 'sweeten' their life. Maddy's owner admitted that the family were having a very tough time and she was very grateful of her grandmother's sentiments. A lovely cob called Saracen showed his lovely owner sitting with a beautiful fluffy cat curled up on her lap. He told me that this cat was in spirit but still liked to lie on his owner's lap. When I told the owner what Saracen had said, we had the inevitable tears, and she said that she knew her cat was still with her and often thought that she felt his presence on her lap.

One of the greatest gifts our animals give us is the gift of tears. As humans we are expert at burying our emotions where they may fester and cause physical symptoms if not released. Animals facilitate such a surge of emotion that we can access these long buried feelings and bring them to the surface to be released. There are very few days when I am working with animals and their owners when there are no tears. At least one owner usually has a good sob, and sometimes it is me, when I am overcome with the love our animals are showing us. It can take weeks of counselling to get a person to acknowledge some grief or deep rooted issue, but a few words from an animal and everything can come to the surface to be healed. This is why many horses are now working in equine assisted therapy with fantastic results with their human patients.

Prima

Another way I have experienced healing with animals is through dreams and out of body experiences. I was working with the sickest horse I had ever seen, called Prima. We discovered later that she had contracted Louping Ill. This is a very nasty disease spread by ticks. Prima lived on a Devon sheep farm where ticks were rife. Her normally sturdy chestnut frame was melting as the disease ravaged her system. Her balance was terrible and she fell so heavily that she knocked the side of the wooden stable out and badly floundered and thrashed on the stable floor. I was really worried at her appearance and really doubted if she could be saved. Her legs trembled as she struggled to stand. She seemed fearful of lying down as if she knew that she might never be able to stand again. He eyes were glazed and sunken with pain, as though she had the worst migraine headache imaginable. She seemed to be teetering on the edge of a precipice. I visualized sending golden energy through her body and gently worked on relieving the pain in her head. She looked slightly relieved but I promised to continue working on her at a distance when I got home. Poor Prima couldn't lower her head to eat or drink and even if water or titbits were placed near or in her mouth, she was still unable to chew or make the painful effort of drinking. She was given an intensive course of antibiotics and was drenched with re-hydrating electrolytes, but she was hanging on by a thread. For three nights her owners nursed her with the hunt kennel man on standby to come and put her out of her misery if it was felt that it was too cruel to prolong this terrible condition. I kept in close contact with her owners and Dave the shaman and I did all we could as a combined effort to help to save her.

Our horse Troy valiantly worked remotely, tending to her pain and gave her healing. Very early on the fourth day at about five o'clock in the morning, I was asleep in bed and I dreamt that Prima had managed to lower her head slightly and drink some much needed water. It seemed so real, I could hear her slurping up the life-giving fluid. I awoke and prayed so hard that this might be true and that she was feeling well enough to drink. I couldn't contain my curiosity any longer and rang the owners, who I knew would be up and about and caring for Prima. I was amazed to be told that Prima had indeed drunk water for the first time since her illness, at exactly the time she showed me in my dream. From then on she went from strength to strength and made a slow but full recovery, much to the delight of us all. Prima had never developed a taste for peppermints before Troy worked with her but I think not all his influences were necessarily good. He has a dreadful peppermint addiction and will 'mug' anyone who has some in their pockets. Since Troy's healing endeavours, Prima has developed a similar interest. However, I feel it is a small price to pay as he was instrumental in her salvation and everyone is so thankful that Prima recovered and she thoroughly deserved some sweet treats at having such a strong will to live.

Gulliver's Travels

Another dream I had was of a very lame three day event horse called Gulliver. He was competing at the prestigious Badminton Horse Trials. He belonged to my friends' son and they were so thrilled because he had finished his second day in the lead of an international field of competitors and was all set to win the event.

However, at the vet's inspection at the end of the day he was pronounced lame and probably unfit to continue, and his whole career as a top international event horse was in doubt. I received a telephone plea asking for help and said I would do my best to help. As I lay in bed I tried to think of healing energy pouring into his tendon, but unfortunately I was so tired I fell asleep. I had the most curious dream that was so vivid I awoke expecting to find myself covered in horsey smells and straw. I dreamt that I was lying underneath him, cradling his injured foreleg. I visualized placing carbon implants into his tendon and saw them strengthening and reenergising all the tissue. I then saw him eventually stand up and trot about, appearing to be completely sound.

I switched on the television that afternoon to see if Gulliver was competing in the televised event, but unfortunately he had definitely been withdrawn. I was so disappointed as my dream had seemed so real and I felt sure that something must have happened and that he had benefited in some way. I rang my friends to enquire how Gulliver was and if they had heard any news. I told them about my dream and they said that their son had rung and said that to their amazement, the horse was much improved by the next morning, but they had withdrawn him as they didn't want to risk his future. He might have been able to compete and possibly win, but he might have paid too high a price and done irreparable damage to his leg. So they wisely allowed him to recover and continue his career when he was fully fit. The next day I heard he was bouncing round like a two year old and they were trying to quieten him to rest his leg.

Positive Healing Tool

Positive visualization is a very powerful healing tool. Sitting in quiet meditation is always a great way to gain access to your higher consciousness that knows everything about communication! The power of your intent is all important. We use so little of our minds on a day to day basis, if we care to delve into deeper realms of subconscious wisdom; there are no limits to our healing abilities, both for ourselves and others.

I worked with a pony called Logan. He seemed completely unwilling to canter and had come to Jenny's yard for re-schooling. He showed me past lives, once as a trotter and once as an Icelandic pack horse, carrying heavy loads of caribou. Neither of these lifetimes warranted the cantering gait and having ridden a retired trotter I knew they would not canter at any price, they would just trot faster and faster. So I asked the two young girls who owned him and their rather sceptical mother to visualize him cantering perfectly. I then asked Jenny to imagine Logan cantering round the school effortlessly, before they went into the school. She promised she would comply with my instructions and everybody committed to doing their homework. The next time Jenny took Logan into the school, she had seen him in her mind's eye cantering round in beautifully balanced circles. Lo and behold, they started some gentle warm up exercises and then Logan promptly broke into an effortless canter. There were cheers all round! He also gave me the most wonderful kiss in thanks for helping him!

As with the case of Nick and Lily, where Nick had visualised all the routes that they would travel with no fear, just happy hacks, that is what they encountered. It is as if we can programme our thoughts for positive outcomes. Athletes use these techniques to great success as they literally picture themselves jumping higher or racing faster and thundering across the winning line. This is just harnessing the power of the mind, which is an awesome tool.

CHAPTER 11

Love Never Dies

Almost every day I spend working with clients and their animals, we are touched and deeply moved by the depth of the animal's connection with their owner. The lengths they are willing to go to find their way back to us phenomenal, and the hardships that they agree to endure, before incarnating; just to help us on our path is awe inspiring.

Pillow Talk

Pillow is another very special dog that has helped me so profoundly on my soul's journey, rather like Mulberry has for Cameron. In fact I have felt her presence and guidance throughout the whole process of this book, so she deserves to be introduced to you in this final chapter.

I had been called to work with a lady's horse in a nearby village and we had some very positive results with the horse's emotional and physical well being, so the owner asked if I worked with people as well. I said that I did indeed work with people's physical and emotional challenges and would be happy to help in any way I could. She mentioned that her husband had been suffering with backache and asked if there was anything I could do to help release the pain. I said I would pay a visit to their home and do my best to help. There had been two lovely dogs running around the stable yard with the most amazing markings. They were long haired Blue Merle collies. I remarked on their unusual markings and what lovely dogs they were; apparently they were mother and son.

I arrived at the house and worked on the husband's back,

which seemed to ease his discomfort and then there suddenly came lots of squeaking and general commotion from next door's garden. As it was such a warm day the patio doors were open, so any external sound could be heard. They told me the male collie had been fraternizing with their neighbours' collie bitch and she had recently given birth to a large litter of puppies. The bitch was a border collie with the more common black and white markings, but he said the puppies were lovely and many had the beautiful Blue Merle colouring. I knew if I went into the garden and took one look at them I would want one, so remarkably for me, refrained from looking. However, I was attending a meditation group at the time and one of the participants had been devastated with the death of her much loved dog, so I promised to put them in touch with the owner of the bitch who was having trouble finding suitable homes for all the puppies. Unfortunately the people who were looking for a puppy didn't think the puppies were suitable because they would be too lively with their collie parentage. I was disappointed as I knew this would have been a doting family for one of the pups. The remaining pups were being sent to a rescue centre as no new homes had been found for the remaining pups and I knew these lively healthy puppies may be put down. That was it, I determined to visit the house and ask for a pup the next day. There was something driving me to home one of them. However, when I had arrived at the house I had missed them by minutes; they had already been collected by the rescue centre and were already on their way. I jumped in the car and

 drove to the centre and was shown the three remaining pups. One was black and white, another was fluffy with nice markings, but the last pup seemed to choose me. She was gorgeous, quite smooth haired, with the most wonderful differing shades of

Pillow

grey in splodges and spots on a white furry background. The rescue centre had just given them names in case they would be adopted and this one was called Penny. I promptly put my name down for her and arranged to collect her as soon as she could be released. Poor little thing, she was so frightened at the trauma of leaving her mum and the awful sad persistent barking that seems to emanate from those places as unhappy dogs pray for a new loving home.

Unfortunately a nasty kennel cough type bug seemed to be doing the rounds in the kennels so collection was delayed until their quarantine period had elapsed. On the day we were allowed to collect her at last, my mother and I drove in excited anticipation to collect the pup. I had worked quite hard persuading my husband that it would be great to have another dog even though we had my Border terrier pup Teazle and an old working collie called Dusty. He was not totally convinced, but he knew it was useless to try to deny giving this needy creature a home and gave in to the idea of having our menagerie enlarged once again.

The poor little pup was so traumatized by her previous journey, when she was torn away from her mother, that she was terrified in the car and was quite car sick. I didn't know the techniques that I do now and was sad at her fear. My mother cuddled her all the way home and she was introduced to Teazle and Dusty who was the matriarch. Teazle, who was totally enigmatic, bounced on her, making instant friends and reassuring her that life could be fun. We renamed her because of Teazle's curious behaviour. We had a linoleum floor in the kitchen that she felt it was quite cold to sit on when she was not in her basket with blankets. So she decided to use the new puppy to sit on. The puppy's head could be seen poking out from beneath Teazle, as she used her body as a soft pillow. She was so good natured that she didn't seem to mind and indeed she was the cuddliest little soul so her new name Pillow, just stuck. She seemed to enjoy nothing more than snuggling into us, and everybody fell in love with her. There was one occasion when Cameron stayed home from infant school because he had a bad cold and cough and was feeling miserable. He and Pillow spent most of the day cuddled up on the couch and I knew that she was administering to her patient by being a soft pillow for him to rest his fevered head.

Cameron and Pillow

Pillow became an integral part of our family life and we decided to move to a large farmhouse on the Somerset Levels with a huge garden and enough ground for Mulberry the goat. It had a lovely L-shaped stable yard which Dusty monitored as she slept in the stable next to Mulberry. Pillow was very destructive in her chewing stages of her puppy hood, despite bones and chews she decided to chew off all the plastic buttons on my cooker (we had wondered what these mangled little pieces of black plastic were, until I went to switch on the cooker!) She also chomped through chair and table legs and wooden knobs on my prized Welsh dresser. So we decided to allow her to sleep in the warm stable at night with Dusty, so she could not destroy anything else when she was unmonitored at night time. I felt so guilty as it seemed so unfair that Teazle should remain indoors, but Pillow was fast wrecking our possessions and we had no utility room.

We had decided to allow Teazle to have puppies and she produced a lovely litter of beautiful pedigree pups and unlike Pillow's cross-bred brothers and sisters, there was a waiting list for this popular breed. My husband had stated categorically that we would not be keeping any of the pups as we had more than enough dogs already and I begrudgingly agreed. I knew that I had chosen very loving homes for the pups and they would have happy lives together with their new owners. Pillow was renamed Auntie Pillow as she lovingly washed the pups after their feeds. Not entirely selfless as they probably tasted delicious, as they were usually covered with the remnants of their minced beef and goat's milk gruel! She was such a dear and once she had finished her terrible teething escapades, she snuggled down in the kitchen next to the cordoned off 'puppy pad' and Teazle seemed glad of her help and was happy to share her puppies with their doting 'aunt'.

Warning Premonition

One night I had an awful premonition. I was 'shown' a dog lying dead and I was told very emphatically by my guides, that I was only just starting to acknowledge, that I must not keep one of Teazle's pups. All of the puppies were gorgeous of course and the runt of the litter was called Wilf. He used to lie on my chest in the evenings as I watched television, on his back like a little dead fly, completely relaxed with his legs akimbo! He had the biggest character and personality of the whole litter and we were all falling for him and sorely tempted to keep him. I had not been shown a clear picture of the dog, just a terrible warning. I was stupid enough to ignore this warning. I turned it around in my head that it could have been one of the puppies that might not be happy in the new home and contrived to believe this might be Wilf so that I could convince myself he should stay.

On the day when a lovely owner was coming to spend time with the chosen puppy, my husband was tiling the kitchen floor, so Pillow was put outside in the garden with Dusty to run around the garden and to keep out of the way of the bonding session. Cameron was playing outside on his toy tractors and all seemed fine. We had finally decided that we might keep Wilf, as he was so adorable and we had made up our minds that morning. Half an hour into the visit from the prospective owner, Cameron came running in shouting that Pillow had been hit by a motorbike and she was lying in the road outside our long driveway that ended with a closed five barred gate. At first I dismissed him, as we had very good fencing in the garden and I couldn't see how it could possibly be Pillow as there didn't seem any way she could get out of our garden. But when I looked down the driveway I could see cars backing up in the road as though there was something blocking the road. Still disbelieving, I ran down the driveway to see what was going on. To my horror there was Pillow lying motionless and several yards down the road a motorcyclist and his bike were spread across the road. This road was normally very quiet, it was only busy during work and school runs in the morning and late afternoon. In my shock I still stared at Pillow not understanding how she could have got out; this couldn't really be happening. My mind could not accept that our wonderful dog was dying in front of me. With my previous veterinary experience I knew she was fading fast and I was devastated to feel her heart beat fade as she laid there not breathing, and then she was gone. We were all completely stunned. I couldn't cry, I couldn't speak, and it just seemed inconceivable that this could have happened. She must have jumped the gate but had never previously attempted such a thing, but to choose that particular time when the road was dangerous seemed so crazy to me. We buried her in the orchard with my husband's woolly hat that she had loved to steal to snuggle into when he was at work, whilst she waited for his return. Teazle was thrown into total grief as we all were and she rushed around the house trying to find her friend, which made us all even more distraught. The guilt I felt was crucifying, when I thought of the warning I had been given and had chosen to ignore. How could I have been so stupid, but was it such a crime to fall for Wilf and somehow engineer his future with us? I felt we had more than enough love to give all the dogs. But I felt I had totally failed Pillow and this awful outcome was my fault. I decided to let Wilf go to the owners that were very eager to home him and commit to finding another rescue dog that really needed a home, in memory of Pillow. Teazle was so distraught and pined dreadfully. She seemed to go into a deep decline as we all were and for days she maintained her search for Pillow, as the pups were slowly collected by their new owners. Her pups were old enough to take care of themselves and she was relieving herself of motherly duties unaided by her former friend.

The strangest thing was that we heard of a puppy that had been picked up by the dog warden in a very rough area of the local town and this was how we found Winnie. What was amazing was that we later found out that she had been picked up at almost exactly the time that Pillow had been killed, which seemed quite strange at he time.

It took a very long time to come to terms with life without Pillow. We still couldn't believe what had happened. We had always had dogs until they were old grey and ancient and had lived long happy lives with us. Pillow was still so young and had her whole life ahead of her and we never doubted that we would have many many, happy years together.

This all happened in the years where I was very slowly being awakened to my spiritual path and in hindsight, I can now see the hard lessons that I was learning. We continued our lives trying to give Winnie and all our animals the best home we could. Teazle seemed to thrive again in Winnie's company and our lives continued.

Reawakening the Temple Priestess
I had looked into the possibilities of past life issues with myself after discovering Cameron's past traumas and I during a meditation I had seen myself in a temple which seemed Egyptian. There I had met a handsome man and we had galloped off together into the sunset on beautiful Arab horses. This was one

meditation that I was reluctant to return from as it was so romantic. I never gave it much thought afterwards, but two years later I was experiencing a regression with a friend of mine and I saw the temple again and I learnt that I had been a high priestess working as a healer in the temple of Karnak. I had never heard of Karnak; I was fascinated by all things Egyptian, but I had never studied the different temples or areas. A week later I received a copy of a mind body spirit book club magazine and on the back pages were advertisements for courses and holidays. To my amazement there was an advert saying "To all the priests and priestesses of Karnak – come and reclaim your ancient wisdom" I nearly fell over as I tingled from head to toe, just knowing that I had to go to Egypt to see if this was true.

When I arrived at Karnak I thought I must have been mistaken after all as I didn't recognize anything from the front entrance and its avenue of sphinxes. However, as I walked further into the temple complex, I knew exactly where I was and where I was going. I recognized the side entrance and pillared columns and the left turn that would lead me into the holy of holies where I had seen large stone plinth that I had laid on years before in my meditation. Once inside the sacred building I started to shudder at the memory of my failing to fulfill my healing duties by abandoning my work in favour of a life with my lover. I had seen in my regression that I had loved him deeply but had always carried enormous guilt for leaving my healing work. I knew that in this incarnation I had to fulfill my duty and never again forsake my soul purpose.

There was a statue dedicated to the Egyptian god Khepri and it was prophesised that if you walked around the statue seven times, your wish would come true. So I thought I'd give it a try. I was asking to be shown the best way forward in my healing and that it be for the very highest good. On my second or third circuit of the statue, I was astounded to find Pillow dominating my mind, and I could see her clearly wagging her tail and looking very happy. This was emotional enough, but when she went on to tell me that she had died in order to address my issues with guilt, it was almost too much to bear. She told me I had carried this through many lifetimes since my Egyptian life possibly 3000 years before and now it was the time to finally let go and resume my healing skills and fulfill my purpose. The rest of the group that I had met were shocked at my floods of tears as I tried to tell them what had occurred. My whole week in Egypt was very emotional as I remembered so much of my previous lives there.

A year later I returned to Karnak with two other members of the group that also shared lifetimes with me and we had decided to return to further deepen our connections with that ancient land. Once again I decided to walk around the statue, this time just asking to be shown the best way forward after a very difficult time since my mother's death.

As before, I had no thought of Pillow, I was concentrating on the recent traumas in my life. But there she was again large as life in my mind, jumping around, wagging and laughing at me in her joyous expression. She said I was doing really well with releasing my guilt and that she was very happy in spirit and glad that I was doing the work that I was meant to be after all this time. Again I was in floods of tears with her love that she shared with me, but this time I tried to share her joy. I was so glad to see she was happy and free in spirit. I determined that I would persevere with my healing work and not fail this time in my commitment to be of service to others. I was able to reflect on how I had been kept on track thus far, thanks to the animals.

Death and Rebirth
The most recent visitation from Pillow came when I had spent time communicating with humpback whales off the Dominican Republic, near the Turks and Caicos Islands. I was feeling rather

ill and exhausted and bereft at leaving their energies that had enveloped me during a whole week on the ocean. I was forced to go to my hotel room and compose myself as I felt waves of emotion sweeping through me. I felt nauseous and faint and wondered what on earth was happening to me. As I lay on my bed, Pillow bounced into my thoughts as unexpectedly as before. I lamented her passing and said mentally to her, "Oh you were so lovely, it was so awful losing you, I still can't believe I lost you."

To this I received a severe telling off! "You never lost me, I am *always* with you. I am always around to make sure you are progressing well. You humans get so hung up on the concept of dying and death. There is no death; it's just another part of life and another experience. You really must let go of the sadness and grief. Celebrate love, reconnection and new phases. Animals have a much better understanding of this and accept the rebirth of death."

Her final words were, "All is as it should be, you are learning well. There are no mistakes, you did nothing wrong. It was not your fault." She added: "I came especially to wake up your sense of knowing that guilt has to be released. It eats away at the soul and diminishes your power, as all emotions can do, if they control you."

I felt that Pillow was a very special energy that had chosen her incarnation with me for this very purpose. I asked her if, like Anneka, she might return one day so that we could physically be together again. She said that she hadn't decided yet. She said she liked being in spirit and the freedom she had. She said that she found the physical form quite heavy and restricting and so for now, was content to be pure energy. She felt that she could do greater healing work in this free form.

Gina and Mani a Whale of a Tale!

I arrived in Puerto Plata in the Dominican Republic to spend a few days at a hotel, before catching the boat to live on the ocean and commune with the humpbacks for a whole week immersed in the whale energy. I was so excited, as this had been a life-long ambition and I was eager to meet up with the group and my friend who had organized the trips. I shared those days with a lovely person called Caroline who had booked this trip as a seventieth birthday present to herself. She had waited a little longer than I had to have this once in a lifetime experience and I was full of admiration for her.

My first night was very restless. I was disturbed in my sleep by pictures of an aquatic centre that had recently opened in Puerto Plata. I had seen the adverts at the airport when I arrived and I saw that there were captive dolphins performing daily shows there and there were large letters on the billboards inviting tourists to "swim with dolphins". Having swum with wild dolphins in the Bahamas and the Azores, I hated the thought of dolphins in captivity and abhorred the fact that they were forced to 'entertain' us.

I was being kept awake by dolphins from the aquarium who kept telling me that one of the female dolphins who they called Mani, was sick and needed my help.

I was told that she had a problem with her swim bladder. I had no idea if dolphins had swim bladders – I knew my goldfish did! But maybe it was their way of telling me that she was out of balance. I had vowed that I would not go to the new centre as I didn't want to patronize such an establishment. But the dolphins were so persistent that I knew I would not get any sleep unless I agreed to go to the centre and find Mani. So the next morning I found Caroline and told her of my disturbed night and my cetacean visitors. We found a tour guide and arranged a trip to the aquarium. Our hearts sank as we arrived to find loud speakers announcing the imminent dolphin show and I watched with tears streaming down my face at these wonderful ocean creatures confined to a pool, having to perform for our 'pleasure' doing various tricks. Some people were allowed to hold onto their dorsal fins and be dragged through the water. We felt the dolphins were so degraded and wished that more people could witness the sheer joy and vivacity of wild dolphins in their natural habitat, who could choose to interact or not, with humans on their own terms.

Caroline asked me how I would recognise Mani and I just knew that she would find me if she could, as there were several sets of dolphins working in different pools. We decided we could

Madeleine and dolphin

not endure the thought of the dolphins having to drag us through the water, so we opted for an encounter where people could sit in the pool and meet a dolphin. There were only two dolphins working in this way that day, except one had a baby that was kept away from the humans. I just knew that the mother dolphin was Mani, although her keeper called her Serena. Mentally I asked the dolphins to let Mani find me and assured them that I was there to do all I could. The dolphins were taught to spend time shaking fins with us and splash us and with the lure of a bucket of fish behind each person, they came and leant on our shoulder. As the dolphin came to me to rest on my shoulder I felt her anguish and I knew it was her. I tried so hard to hold her in my arms and give her healing. It was a very special moment and I prayed that she had benefited in some way. As we left the centre after we were shown photographs of our encounters. When I saw the photograph of Mani and me, I decided I had to have a record of our healing exchange.

When I went to bed that night I was feeling very pensive and reflected on the day's events. I tried to recapture the wonderful feeling of a real live dolphin in my arms, their soft rubbery texture of their cool skin, and I hoped that in some way I had helped. Suddenly I felt the weight of her on my shoulder once more. It was as though her energy had returned to give me more information and to get more healing. She explained that she was sad because her baby would never experience freedom. She had become disconnected from source, which is the universal connection to all that is.

I worked as I would normally with an animal, but I imagined placing my hand on her tail and sending energy up through her body. I visualized rebalancing all her physical chakras, which were similar to ours, but I was amazed to be told that a dolphin has twelve higher chakras and she told me that a Baleen whale like a humpback has 21 chakras! These soul chakras are linked directly into the planetary grids, but until Mani explained this I had no idea just how important the whales were.

As I helped her release her sadness I realized that she had become disconnected because of her fear and sadness for her baby. She had forgotten that captivity can be just a frame of mind and that she could reconnect with the universe and 'travel' anywhere she wanted to, in fact she could not only bi-locate (which means being in two places at once energetically) but multi-locate. This is the concept that we can astral travel and 'journey' to many places and dimensions, outside of our normal physical confines.

She remembered that she could teach her baby this and so she left me filled with happiness. I realized that this had occurred in what Aborigines call the 'dream time' and in the last whispers of my dream time that night, she came again, lightly resting on my right shoulder and proceeded to send electrifying energy through my body. It was so powerful I felt my whole body shuddering, it was almost startling. I felt such gratitude from her and she said that she was thanking me and preparing me for the more powerful energies of the whales, who I was about to encounter.

I told Caroline about my wonderful night and we reflected that perhaps the captive dolphins were performing very important tasks. Perhaps they had chosen to work in this way, so that they could reach and touch in some subconscious spiritual way, to re-awaken dormant awareness in people that would not normally seek to advance themselves in that way consciously. Not everyone was as fortunate as Caroline and I having been privileged enough to have swum with wild dolphins. And perhaps this was the only way dolphins could reach the masses. Most tourists viewed their encounters as a bit of fun and something to amuse the kids. Perhaps they were getting far more than they realized from these wonderful creatures.

Gina the Humpback Whale

It's difficult to describe the enormity of the overwhelming awe, that I felt swimming next to a humpback whale. Being out in the ocean for a whole week, surrounded by these incredible creatures was an experience I will never forget and I feel so fortunate to have been able to physically connect with these wonderful caretakers of the planet. Apart from the sheer physical size of these creatures, their energetic presence is mind blowing and life changing. The experience with Mani was powerful enough but it was just a prelude to the power of the energy that was going to permeate by being.

We boarded our boat from the dock in Puerto Plata and travelled about eight hours out into the ocean in an area called the Silver banks. This is a very special area as it is chosen as a safe calving ground for females to have their young and for the males to find a mate to couple with to complete the cycle. The number of whales at any one time is about 150 so you can imagine what it might have been like living in the midst of all that incredible energy. We travelled out in small inflatable RIBs during the day, which felt very small out in the middle of the ocean, knowing that underneath there were probably 40-feet long whales that could

capsize us in a heart beat. Of course these creatures are incredibly
gentle, and the company that ran these wild encounters were very
respectful and tried at all costs to be non-invasive, especially with
the mothers and their young, newborn calves. They placed us in
the water to swim next to the whales, only when they were
satisfied that the whales were relaxed about our presence. Seeing
these leviathans surfacing and breaching and blowing right next
to us was just sublime. Several males would vie for the female's
attentions and they would have battles by fin slapping or tail
slapping, which was quite a display. One time I was in the water
and four competing males or 'rowdies' were coming straight
towards me. This was quite scary as I could have been swatted
like a tiny fly in the water. However, they were well aware of our
presence and much to my relief they dived beneath us and I
looked down and saw them pass beneath me one by one. Once
they felt it was safe to surface without harming us, they thrust up
in fountains of spray and resumed their titanic battles. Another
time I was snorkelling over a young male that was obviously
feeling lonely and unsuccessful in finding a mate. He was singing

in deep mournful tones and I could feel the sound passing through my body. I could feel it physically affecting me, balancing and harmonizing my physiological systems. I was slightly alarmed when he started to surface right under me and I knew that I would not be able to get out of the way fast enough. But of course I needn't have worried. As he came closer he calculated exactly how close he could come without harming me. We were instructed to remain very still if this happened. I felt very small and insignificant. Instead of rising in their normal humped shape, he kept very flat just beneath me and only when he knew he was clear of me, did he surface and his huge tail or fluke was only inches from my body. This was so incredible; I knew the whale had been so careful not to hurt me, as I could easily have been killed. I thanked him so much for his gentle care and tried to send him so much love from my heart centre, which I prayed he received.

If this profound exchange was not enough to satisfy my life long dream, I was to be blessed with even deeper experiences to hold dear to me forever. On the third day of our oceanic sojourn, we were called to meet up with the other small boat, who had found a mother and calf that seemed very happy to spend time with their human visitors.

She was a huge female and her baby was about three weeks old. Even at this tender age, the calf was no lightweight! It was very curious and spent its time circling our group, staring in what seemed like disbelief at the strange looking wet suited creatures, bobbing around in the water. To be eyeballed by a whale is an experience that goes beyond words. The trust that the mother had for us as she seemed to almost actively encourage the calf to learn about us, was incredible. She allowed groups, to take it in turns to spend time with them for four hours. She was just resting in the water, surfacing about every 25 minutes and sent her calf up to breath about every five to six minutes. She would gently lift the calf up with her huge pectoral fin; he would have a quick gulp of air, perform a tour of the human group and then nestle into his mum for a quick drink of milk.

The water was crystal clear, so we could just float in the water, with our masks and snorkels, witnessing this fantastic display. The sunlight shone down through the water and dappled the whales in light. We were all truly blessed that day.

However, I did not receive profound wisdom from the whales whilst in the water. I think I was too awe struck by their magnificence. It was only when I retired to my bunk at night that the messages came through thick and fast. We could hear the whales all around us at night, surfacing and blowing. In fact, if you were on deck you could be forced to run from one side to the other, so as not to miss another second of a chance to see a humpback in its natural habitat. We were hungry to gather and store as many encounters as possible, to fill life-long memories.

Whales and Planetary Healing

Before travelling to the whales I had been asked by a global network of healers to unite as part of an anchor group, to bring planetary healing. I had said that I would be with the humpbacks and would ask for their help in anchoring in this special energy of love which was called the divine lotus heart energy.

The night before the chosen date of the global connection, I lay in my bunk and reconnected with the mother whale. She laughingly said I could call her Gina. She said she knew how we humans loved to give names to things and needed a 'handle' to communicate. I thanked her from the bottom of my heart, for allowing us to spend time with her and her beautiful baby. She said that she had spent time with us because she wanted to teach and demonstrate to us the deeper concepts of trust. When you consider just how many humpback whales have been killed and still are being slaughtered by man, I found it almost inconceivable that this whale could show so much compassion and love for a species that was single handedly destroying her fellow beings and their environment. She said we needed to believe in trust and to learn to trust ourselves in the deepest meaning of the word.

I recorded the following conversation with Gina, so that I could relate it to you in this book. I hurriedly scribbled down the notes when she had finished so I would not forget a word of her wisdom!

Madeleine: "What do you know of the lotus heart?"

Gina: "The lotus heart cushions the planet. The more you send out love to the planet and send love into yourselves, the more the planet will be lowered into the love and protection of the divine love of the lotus. Visualize the earth, becoming wrapped in the joy and divinity of the one love, encapsulated by the lotus."

Madeleine: "What about the Akashic records, do you hold the keys?"

I wanted to know about this as I had been told that whales are the record keepers for all humanity and these records are called the Akashic records.

Gina: "You all, each and every one of you, hold the key to the wisdom of the Akashic records. The key is held in your heart. In order to turn and open the key, you have to send love to yourself. You appear and feel like a tiny ant, randomly running around.

Your perception is that you are separate, with no purpose. But you must realize that one ant is part of the whole, working to build, strengthen and protect the hill (the earth). Remember the power of the ant to move mountains. You often feel 'what can one person do? What use am I?' Remember the ant and become as one to build the whole."

The amount of compassion and caring that poured out of these words that filled my mind in the small hours of the night, curled up in my bunk, overwhelmed me. It was as though the whale was treating mankind as some kind of wayward, delinquent that had gone off the rails. All that was needed was love and understanding to bring them back on track.

I reflected on her analogy, comparing me to the ant, and I remembered that size for size the ant was capable of moving its mountain equivalent.

I had been feeling isolated and separate, feeling sometimes like a voice in the wilderness. I had the love from the animals, but I wasn't integrating that into myself enough and equating it to self-love. What a gift of awareness Gina gave to me.

Anchoring the Energy

The next day I invited anyone who might be interested to join in the anchoring of the divine lotus heart energy and I described Gina's visualization and what we had to concentrate on. In meditation I had visualized the planet earth. It was floating above a huge lotus with a million petals opened in invitation, for the planet to draw succour from its protection. It was just waiting for the planet to be gently lowered into its centre.

So at the agreed hour, whilst out in the ocean, we concentrated on the planet descending gently into the waiting lotus to be enveloped in its love. I hoped that our combined efforts around the world would help send healing to our ailing planet. I also send out the biggest waves of loving thanks to the whales that I could muster and hoped that Gina would feel my gratitude from her ocean depths. That night I was thrilled to visualize in my meditation, a huge shift in the planet. There, to my amazement, was the earth completely wrapped by the petals of the lotus. Something had happened from all our healing intent and I vehemently prayed that the planet benefited physically.

What was even more astounding for me was that Caroline had lent me a copy of *Animal Voices* by Dawn Baumann Brunke. I had been greatly enjoying reading a book which reiterated by beliefs so beautifully. I had picked the book up to read a few pages after such an amazing, but exhausting day. I was stunned as I read the following passage written by a lady called Penelope Smith, who was describing her impression of a female Orca's energy and tone, whilst communicating with her.

* "The images I get besides this booming tone, is of a great lotus. It comes under the earth and completely supports the earth. The energy goes through the earth and now my heart has turned into this huge lotus, which is the greater love. The biggest message from the whales is to love the greater love. Whales say that from dolphins you learn what love is and from us you learn to love the greater love."

This book was written several years before my trip and here we had an Orca who along with all the other whales, that knew all about the divine lotus heart energy, long before some humans decided that we needed to join forces to visualize this for the planet.

I also reflected on the power of thought to change water molecules in either a positive or negative way. Imagine all the loving energy from the whales being instilled into the oceans that create the biggest mass of the earth's surface area of our 'Blue Planet'.

I learnt similar lesson from giant whale sharks later that year when I swam with them off the coast of Mexico. They were just as in tune with the plight of the planet and generously gave me healing meditations that connected the Mayan pyramid at Chichen Itza to the Great Pyramid at Giza. I visited the Mayan site and received yet more help and advice to implement my visualisations from the whale sharks.

I hope that the messages from these majestic creatures are enough to impact on and change what seems to be Man's rush to self destruct and destroy our beautiful planet.

I am humbled by their willingness to heal us and to guide us back to the path of love.

Epilogue

Before visiting the whales and experiencing my healing from Mani and my telling off from Pillow, I seemed to come to some kind of impasse with the writing of this book.

I encountered a form of performance anxiety in my fear that people would not believe or be able to relate to my findings. I felt that I would not be able to explain or describe well enough. I forgot to ask the animals to help. When I re-read my first attempts, I realized it was too I orientated. How conceited of me. I now realise just how much healing I have received from the animals, as they have lovingly nurtured, cajoled, laughed and sighed in exasperation at my doubts and deliberations. Pillow and Gina promised that they would help me write and finish the book and so I have drawn upon their wisdom, to remind me of all the wonderful animals that have been my tutors along the way, for which I am eternally grateful. I truly hope that you will allow the messages and teachings of the animals to flow through you, so that you can draw from this book what you will. I had lots of help and so do you.

Just open your heart...

White Buffalo Calf
Flagstaff Arizona Jan 2005

White buffalo calf

... Teaching me about the return of the white buffalo to heal mother earth...

"We are anchoring the life blood into the stones of our mother. She wept at our loss. We come to remind you of what was lost. We come to remind you of what was and how you should honour our mother and yourself. This is our message...

Learn it well."

Acknowledgements

I would like to thank all the people, guides and animals that have been such huge catalysts in my life, it would need several pages to mention you all, but you know who you are! I would especially like to thank Margaret Ellis, who as my polarity therapist first opened my eyes to the possibilities of the universe. Thea Holly gave me so much support before and after my mother's death and connected me to outer planetary healing energies. Leigh Jackson and 'that puppy' Sam, who introduced me to Judith Webster, the holistic vet who has been so supportive and encouraging, and who introduced me to the wonderful Julie Dicker, a pioneer in animal communication, now watching over us from spirit. Leigh also was the catalyst in my meeting and working with Dave Maclamont and Troy. His team of helpers join forces with me on the really serious cases that we encounter. His spirit dogs Rab and Rock help Pillow and I with our difficult canine SOS cases. Gnesius, the dragon, who helps with negative auras and the Takaren, outer planetary beings, that advise us. Troy has now returned to Dave, as he was not ready to retire quite yet, and is a wonderful healing ally for us all. He and Mulberry still confer to give the best advice. Huge thanks to Jenny and Tony Boon who have allowed me to work and treat people and animals at their farm. Big thanks to Kay Williams in Australia for creating my websites. I would also like to thank Jenny Smedley for all her help and encouragement and technical support as I am such a technophobe. She has been so tireless in helping me promote my work, to get the message of the animals heard. She guided my tentative first steps into writing this book with her invaluable advice from her prolific writing experience and she put me in contact with my publisher O Books. And of course my thanks to John Hunt at O Books who has given me this chance to get the concept of "An Exchange of Love" 'out there'. Carolyn Burdet helped so much with her article about my work in Kindred Spirit magazine, that spread the word both nationally and internationally; and the stories and cases of animals reincarnating to be with their owners again, and of healing horses' shattered blueprints, have developed into this book. I also need to thank her for doing such a great job with editing this book, so that I hope I have created something that the animals will approve of!

I am eternally grateful to you all.

Useful Contacts

Madeleine Walker works as an animal intuitive and healer, horse and rider trauma consultant, healer and empowerment coach and as a holistic stress management consultant for people. She runs workshops on animal communication and healing, and emotional release through art. For details of her clinics and courses or to arrange a consultation, see www.anexchangeoflove.com and www.gatewaystothelight.com

For postal readings send a photograph of the animal and its name with a tuft of its hair/fur to PO Box 782, Taunton, TA1 9YB, England, UK. Please include your name and address and email contact and telephone number. There is a consultation fee for this work.

Judith Webster is a practicing homeopathic vet, specialising in equine care, with 25 years experience. She uses homeopathy primarily in all cases, and conventional medicine and natural therapies where needed. Judith Webster Veterinary Surgeon, Raddon Barton, Lydford, Devon, EX20 4BP, England, UK. email judith@webster6231.freeserve.co.uk or mobile tel (+44) (0)7785972291. When relevant she may refer cases to other therapists for treatment such as Bowen, equine osteopathy, acupuncture, dentistry, and healing.

Kat Middleton Fd Sc, is a natural horsemanship trainer who trains people to connect to their horses by understanding the power of body language. For information on lectures, demonstrations and training for you and your horse with Natural Horsemanship Equine Behaviour and Training see www.info@lydfordhouse.com
or email middleton557@btinternet.com mobile tel (+44) 7870944819.

Bibliography

* With kind permission, quote from; / Animal Voices/ by Dawn Baumann Brunke, Bear & Company, Rochester, VT 05767
   Copyright © 2002 Inner Traditions / Bear & Company, Inc. www.BearandCompany.com published by Bear and Co.

BOOKS

O books
O is a symbol of the world, of oneness and unity. In
different cultures it also means the "eye", symbolizing
knowledge and insight, and in Old English it means "place
of love or home". O books explores the many paths of
understanding which different traditions have developed
down the ages, particularly those today that express
respect for the planet and all of life.

For more information on the full list of over 300 titles
please visit our website
www.O-books.net

SOME RECENT O BOOKS

Forever Faithful
Dogs That Return
Jenny Smedley

Enchanting. Jenny's true-live(s) story of her beloved dog and horse are a must read for every person who has ever loved, and been loved, by an animal companion. **Rae Ann Kumelos**, Voice of the Animal

978-1-84694-174-0 160pp **£9.99 $19.95**

Striking at the Roots
A Practical Guide to Animal Activism
Mark Hawthorne

Brilliant, easy to read, full of real-life experiences and practical examples. If you want to make your life count, influence others and save a few thousand lives, this book is your roadmap. Give it to everyone you know! **Ingrid Newkirk**, president of People for the Ethical Treatment of Animals

9781846940910 304pp **£9.99 $19.95**

Reiki Meditations for Beginners
with free CD
Lawrence Ellyard

One of the few Reiki books which really covers something new and valuable. Reiki and Meditation is a core topic for everyone who likes to

use Usui-Reiki as a spiritual path. This is why Mikao Usui emphasized so much to meditate every morning and every evening. A must read for every serious Reiki-Practitioner! **Walter Lübeck,** co-author of *The Spirit of Reiki*

9781846940989 176pp **£12.99 $24.95**

The Celtic Wheel of the Year
Celtic and Christian Seasonal Prayers
Tess Ward

This book is highly recommended. It will make a perfect gift at any time of the year. There is no better way to conclude than by quoting the cover endorsement by Diarmuid O'Murchu MSC, "Tess Ward writes like a mystic. A gem for all seasons!" It is a gem indeed.
Revd. John Churcher, Progressive Christian Network

1905047959 304pp **£11.99 $21.95**

Gays and the Future of Anglicanism
Andrew Linzey and Richard Kirker

This book breathes toleration. It invites thought. It abhors the polemical. It is very Anglican - in the best sense - in that it tries to bring under-standing, be inclusive and avoid expulsion. Yet it has authority, without being bossy and authoritarian. Readers will find much to chew on to help them think about what is the nature of church for which they strive. "Gays and the Future of Anglicanism" is about much more than homosexuality and is highly recommended.
RENEW

190504738X 384pp **£17.99 $29.95**

A Global Guide to Interfaith
Reflections From Around the World
Sandy Bharat

This amazing book gives a wonderful picture of the variety and excitement of this journey of discovery.
Rev Dr. Marcus Braybrooke, President of the World Congress of Faiths

1905047975 336pp **£19.99 $34.95**

God in the Bath
Relaxing in the Everywhere Presence of God
Stephen Mitchell

This little book is destined to become a spiritual classic...A wonderfully refreshing and invigorating reading of Christianity.
Nigel Leaves, author of *Odyssey*

1905047657 112pp **£9.99 $19.95**

God Without God
Western Spirituality Without the Wrathful King
Michael Hampson

Writing with an admirable lucidity and following a tight line of argument, Michael Hampson outlines a credible Christian theology for the twenty-first century. Critical at times of both evangelical and catholic traditions, of both liberal and conservative thinking, he seeks to make faith accessible to those for whom established forms of belief have

become inappropriate in the present-day context.
Canon David Peacock, former Pro-Rector, University of Surrey

9781846941023 256pp **£9.99 $19.95**

Gospel of Falling Down
The beauty of failure, in an age of success
Mark Townsend

It's amazing just how far I was drawn into Mark's words. This wasn't just a book but an experience. I never realized that failure could be a creative process.
Editor, '*Voila*' Magazine

1846940095 144pp **£9.99 $16.95**

Liberal Faith in a Divided Church
Jonathan Clatworthy

This is a truly radical book, in that it looks for the roots of a liberal approach to Christianity that is principled, inclusive and undogmatic. Jonathan Clatworthy shows how liberal faith has always striven to temper the wisdom of the past with the promptings of the Spirit in the present. Rather than seeing such an approach as a departure from true orthodoxy, he demonstrates that they lie at the heart of a consistent vision of God's relationship with the world. This book will provide encouragement and sustenance for those who wish for an alternative to absolute certainty, in its secular and religious forms.
Elaine Graham, Professor of Social and Pastoral Theology, University of Manchester

9781846941160 272pp **£14.99 $29.95**